MOVIN' ON UP

Columbia Records

MOVIN' ON UP

by
Mahalia Jackson

with Evan McLeod Wylie

Hawthorn Books, Inc.
Publishers
New York

First Edition: November, 1966

Portions of this book first appeared in *The Saturday Evening Post,* copyright © 1959 by Curtis Publishing Company, and in *Good House-keeping,* copyright © 1961 by the Hearst Corporation. Used with permission.

Speech by Dr. Martin Luther King used with permission of the Southern Christian Leadership Conference.

Acknowledgment is made for permission to use lines from "We Shall Overcome," copyright 1960 and 1963 by Ludlow Music, Inc.

Second Printing: December, 1966

With the grace of God
I dedicate this book
to my late Aunt Mahalia Paul
and all children everywhere.

Contents

1	Rise up singing	11
2	Somewhere listening	29
3	One step toward the Lord	39
4	Come on, children, let's sing!	51
5	I'm going to live the life I sing about	60
6	Always look up	70
7	Movin' on up	80
8	Keep your hand on the plow	90
9	Going home	103
10	I been 'buked	118
11	The Star-Spangled Banner	132
12	Tell the world about this	140
13	Keep a-movin'	155
14	Walk in Jerusalem	164
15	If we never needed the Lord before	173
16	We shall overcome!	186
17	Just as I am	206
	Discography	215
	The Co-Author and the Book	221

MOVIN' ON UP

1
Rise up singing

Ever since I began singing in the big concert halls, people have been trying to teach me to be grand, but I just can't do it. Some folks get so grand that you can't hand them a letter from home, but I just don't know how they can get that way. If blessings come to you, accept them, but don't let them dominate you.

When I get to New York City and sing at Madison Square Garden and at Carnegie Hall I feel like a peacock with all my feathers spread out; but when I get back to Sixty-third Street in Chicago and look down at my feet all those feathers drop. I remember then that I've been singing now for almost forty years and most of the time I've been singing for my supper as well as for the Lord.

It's hard for me sometimes to believe I came from the back streets of New Orleans and now I have people sitting in the aisles and listening to my gospel songs. When I cry when I'm singing, I am not sad the way people think. I look back and see where I came from, and I rejoice.

I was born on Water Street in New Orleans in 1911—between the railroad tracks and the levee of the Mississippi River. The railroad ran so close that the trains shook the windows. It was a mixed-up neighborhood, with Negroes, French, Creoles and Italians all trying to scratch out a liv-

11

ing. The Negro men in the neighborhood worked around the river, on the docks and the steamboats and the banana boats. My father moved cotton on the river docks in the daytime, barbered people at night and preached on Sundays. He made enough to get along, but we never had much money.

We lived in a little old "shotgun" shack. It rained about as much inside our house as it did outside, and we were always putting out pots and pans to catch the water and sweeping it out with brooms, but those floors were always scrubbed clean.

My papa's father lived just around the corner. Both my grandparents had been born into slavery, on a rice plantation about a hundred miles from New Orleans. After the Civil War was over they were set free, but they stayed on for a while. My grandfather used to tell us about how when he finally got ready to leave he just picked up and walked on into New Orleans on his two feet. That's how Negroes got around in those days. They still do in some parts of the South.

My mother's family was the Clarks. For a long, long time they had lived way up north from New Orleans, on a white man's cotton plantation on the Chafalaye River. During the days of slavery my great-grandmother had been a cook on the plantation and my great-grandfather had been a coachman. My mother's father got to be a foreman and handled the ginning and baling of the cotton before it was loaded on steamboats to go down the Chafalaye River to the Mississippi and New Orleans.

The plantation was called the "Gumpstump Plantation" and it was owned by Captain D. T. Merrick, who had fought with the Confederate Army during the Civil War. After the slaves were freed, the Gumpstump place had become a sharecropper plantation. The Merricks raised cotton with Negroes and mules. The Negroes did the planting and hoeing and the cotton picking and the mules did the plowing.

My grandparents lived in a little log cabin on the Merrick plantation. They cooked over a wood-burning fireplace. They chinked the floor cracks with rags and they took barrel hoops and decorated them with colored paper and bits of cloth for decorations for their home. They farmed a little patch of that rich black buckeye soil you find up there in Pointe Coupee Parish to raise some vegetables. In the autumn my grandfather used to slaughter his hogs and salt down the pork and smoke the bacon. They lived and died in that same cabin and they raised and fed fifteen children.

I can reach back into my memory and hear Uncle Porter, my mother's oldest brother, tell about how he grew up there and how the colored people were treated. He still believes that God put a curse on that part of the South where the white people robbed the colored people for the cotton. He remembers the white men riding those fine-blooded saddle horses around the plantation while the colored men, women and children got fifty cents a day for chopping and picking cotton in the hot sun.

The big plantation bell would ring at four o'clock in the morning, Uncle Porter told us, and the colored men and boys were supposed to be out in the fields by daylight. They plowed behind the mules from sunup until sundown to earn seventy-five cents a day, but the money was mostly kept on the books at the plantation store. The store sold the sharecropping Negroes barrels of pickled pork and corn meal and molasses, but the way the accounts were kept they saw to it that a colored man never got caught up on what he owed. If a Negro bought a mule on time to plow a little for himself on his own patch of land, he kept on paying and paying for that mule and ten years later they would tell him, "No, you don't own that mule yet."

In those days it was compulsory for the white children to go to school but the colored children only went to school when it rained. On days when the sun shone they were supposed to be out in the field chopping cotton. The colored school only went as far as the fifth grade because the teacher only knew how to teach up that far himself, and the white people didn't want to have the colored going any higher anyway.

They were a proud and selfish people, those plantation owners, and I believe that Uncle Porter is right—that God finally sent the boll weevil to jumble them. When the boll weevil came, it ate right through thousands of fields of cotton and most of those big plantations went bankrupt. That part of the South went down and it has never come back up. Thanks to the boll weevil, a lot of those thieving plantation people died out, too.

Way out there in the deep country, the only social life for the colored people was in their church. They had an old slave-built church called St. John's Baptist Church. It was over a hundred years old and made from sawmill cypress planks. When it came time for baptism, the preacher baptized the congregation in the Chafalaye River where the currents ran so swift that they could turn a steamboat around. Uncle Porter was baptized and confirmed in that deep, swift-running river and he has always said that the memory of that day has never left him. He has always felt the spirit of it and recalls the way it made him feel a part of God's human family for the rest of his life.

Uncle Porter had changed the lives of all of us. He had brought my mother and her sisters and brothers down the Mississippi River to New Orleans from the country. He made his first trip down the river about 1890, when McKinley was President of the United States and when New Orleans had a waterfront of tall-stacked steamboats nine miles long.

My uncle was one of the brightest colored boys on that part of the river, and he wanted to better himself. When he was just ten years old, he asked Captain Merrick for a pair of shoes.

14

"Boy," said Captain Merrick, "you don't need any shoes. Go grease your legs! That will keep them warm in the winter and shiny in the summer!"

After that, Uncle Porter vowed he would find a way to leave that plantation life. He used to play around the river levee watching the U. S. Army Corps of Engineers river boats that were charting the river bottom. Whenever anybody heaved a line to tie up to the riverbank, Uncle Porter was right there to catch it and help the men tie up the boat. After a while the engineers gave him a job on the boat.

A white steamboat captain from New Orleans took Uncle Porter under his wing. Captain Rucker was as different from the Merricks as day is from night. He called my uncle "my colored son" and he practically brought him up himself right alongside his own children. To this day, when Uncle Porter goes back to New Orleans to visit them, they call him their "colored brother." One of his best friends is Captain Buddy Rucker, who became a Mississippi River pilot and now is the captain of the excursion boat *The President* that sails out of New Orleans.

On the river Uncle Porter learned to be a cook. He learned over those coal and wood stoves in the galleys of the little steamboats that ran up the small rivers and creeks to the country cotton plantations. He learned how to use a cup of corn meal to settle the muddy river water to the bottom of the water barrel so he could get a dipper of clear water for his bread dough. Later on he sailed on the bigger river boats. He cooked on the *Bessie Anne,* a fast mail boat that ran the Mississippi between Natchez and New Orleans and he worked on stern-wheelers on the Red River and the Chafalaye River from New Orleans to Vicksburg as a chef-cook.

At that time those big steamboats were the queens of the river. They all had beautiful dining rooms and the best of service, and they prided themselves on serving the best food in the land. My uncle Porter got to be a first-class cook, but he also had to learn how to keep out of trouble. Life on the Mississippi among the steamboat crews could be a dangerous life. Everybody carried pistols and dirks in their belts. One little word could lead you into a terrible struggle. I remember hearing about one of my mother's sisters who got into trouble with a mate on one of those steamboats. On a dark night some of the crew threw him overboard and he was never seen or heard from again.

Uncle Porter survived because he always tried to lead his life according to the Word of God. The baptism he had in the Chafalaye River stayed with him. After he got to know Mississippi and New Orleans he went back up to Gumpstump and coaxed his brothers and sisters out of that plantation life one by one. He brought my aunt Duke, my aunt Alice and my aunt Belle into New Orleans. He brought my mother, whose name was Charity, down the river on the steamboat *Julia Anne Partridge*, which carried cotton and passengers from the country. In New Orleans he got her a houseworking job with the family of his friend, Captain Rucker. He's always told me how he remembers my mother as a pretty brown-skinned girl with a sweet disposition. My disposition, he says, is mixed and the best side of it comes from Mother.

After Uncle Porter had brought most of his own family out of that back country, he still wasn't finished. On his trips up the Chafalaye River he coaxed a lot of other young colored boys off the plantations by telling them how they could better themselves and find out there was more to life than chopping cotton. After they got their training as cooks and waiters on the river boats they were ready for jobs on the railroad or in the hotels in the big cities. They never went back again to the plantations. The old folks wouldn't leave. The change was too much for them. But God had stirred Uncle Porter to lead the young people out of the wilderness of that sharecropping existence.

My mother and father met and married in New Orleans, and our family settled around Water Street in the Sixteenth Ward. This section was called the Front of the Town, which meant it was right along the levee on a big bend of the Mississippi River. Behind us was Fontainebleu Drive, where the wealthy white people lived, and beautiful Audubon Park, and the big white-pillared homes of the Garden District. Downtown New Orleans was four miles down the river and children in our neighborhood didn't get to go down there much except on holidays.

The river levee was high and grassy, and it was our playground. We used to sit out there and sing songs with ukuleles and bake sweet potatoes in fires made from driftwood and catch all the fish and shrimp and crabs we wanted. We went every day to church and played there too. We had a Sunday school choir and even when I was tiny my voice was getting so big they let me sing in it.

Some of Papa's folks were in show business. Two cousins —Jeanette Jackson and her husband, Josie Burnette—were traveling with the famous colored singer Ma Rainey, the Mama of the Blues. They had a sort of "Butterbeans and Susie" comedy act with her tent show. The colored show folks didn't have a chance to play in theaters then, and they played anywhere they could in big tents.

Well, the minute my cousins heard that voice of mine, they wanted to get me into show business and they asked my mother to let them take me traveling with them. But my mother wouldn't hear of it. And she didn't have a dime when she said "no" to them either. It's easy to be independent when you've got money. But to be independent when you haven't got a thing—that's the Lord's test. I stayed home, and it changed my whole life.

The people I grew up with in New Orleans were very serious about the church and very devout Christians. In our house we shut everything down from Friday night until

My aunt Duke always worried about me getting mixed up with show business, but I finally convinced her that I am a church woman.

My friends everywhere are so good to me! *Columbia Records*

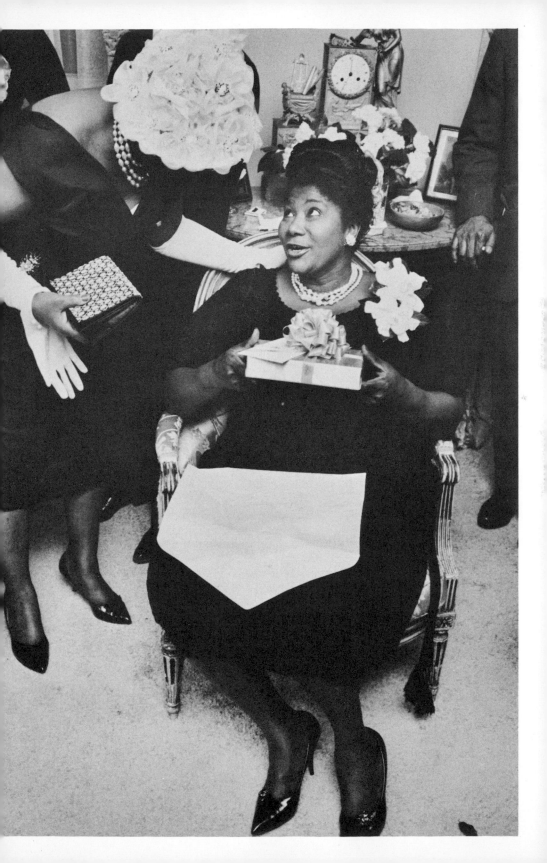

Monday. Either you were a Christian and acted like it or you were put out of the church.

The Baptists still watch me like a hawk, now that I'm mixed up with show business, but they don't have to worry because I still believe in the way they taught me. My strength has always been in the church and I'll never leave it.

I think it's all right for the lay people to have their entertainment but people who are leaders in the church—the inspirational people—they have to lead a careful life. That's the way I was brought up. The preacher lived a clean life. He was a man of God and he lived that way.

The principle of Christianity is right. If we don't apply it, it's a fault of ours, not the Lord. I would not feel deserving of what Christianity has done for me if I did all the things that some people do today. It's gotten to be that people think they have to have everything. I say you can't have it and you don't have any business doing it if you're a Christian.

When I was only five years old, my mother was taken sick. To this day nobody seems to know what the illness was, but in a few months she was dead. They took her back to the country town where our family had come from. I remember a wagon met the train and carried us to the river. They put the casket in a little white skiff and we got in another and they rowed us across to where the country people who had known my mother as a child were waiting to bury her in a little cemetery next to a church. The memory of that little white skiff carrying my mother back home still lives in my mind, but I was too young then to understand sorrow.

On the way back to the city after the funeral the talk began among the relatives about who was going to take care of me and my brother, William, who was ten years old. My mother was one of seven sisters and there was a lot of bickering among the aunts. It was settled quick when the aunt I was named for, Mahalia Paul, spoke up. "I'll take 'em both," she said. And that was that.

Mahalia Paul was known to everybody as Aunt Duke, and she was a power in our family. She was a dark-brown-skinned woman who carried herself very straight and she had gray eyes that looked right through you. She was a high-class cook for a wealthy white family over on St. George Avenue, where the real bluebloods lived, and she ruled her kitchen in the white folks' house and all the other help over there, too. She was such a great cook that she got ten dollars a week, and that was high pay for a colored servant in those days.

Aunt Duke was a power in our neighborhood, too. There was a lot of sporting life among the Negroes in the Sixteenth Ward. There was lottery and games of cotch and skin and there were two saloons only a block away. When a fight started at night you'd hear Aunt Duke shouting, "Get your mess off my premises! Git! Do you hear me!" And those that were doing the scuffling outside got out quick.

When I went to live with Aunt Duke my life was changed. In my own house, I'd been "little Haley," the pet of the family. With my mother lying sick in her bed I'd been running in and out of the house and around the neighborhood doing just as I pleased. Aunt Duke put a stop to all that. She wanted to raise me right for my dead mother's sake, but she had to do it her way. She wasn't one for showing much affection. She believed in the church and hard work and no frills—and little as I was, I had to learn to toe the line. Otherwise she got out the cat-o'-nine-tails. And when she hit you a lick, she got you nine times at once in different places.

The affection in my life had to come from my uncle Emanuel Paul, who was a kindly man, and from my father. Even though I couldn't live with him, I used to visit Papa down at the barbershop where he cut hair in the evening. He'd put me up on his lap and call me his "chocolate drop" and he never scolded me or whipped me. Saturday he would give me what money he could to take back to Aunt Duke for making a home for me.

Aunt Duke didn't believe in fancy clothes. She wore a blue or white uniform when she went to work and kept a best dress for church on Sunday and that was it. I was allowed one dress, and went barefoot all the time. When it came time to get dressed up on Saturday and Sunday, we children used to bathe our legs and then rub them with vaseline to make them shine. We took our baths in the kitchen and heated the hot water on the stove or out in the yard in the sun in one of those big number three tin tubs.

As a child I never had a toy or a store-bought doll. I used to make a rag doll and braid up grass for hair for its head. I never saw a Christmas tree except in our church. I used to hate to leave the church at night at Christmas and see them put the lights out on the tree. I think that's why I have evergreen trees all around my house in Chicago now, so that I can look out the windows and see those beautiful trees all around my yard.

It gets so hot in New Orleans that everybody is up early to work in the cool of early morning. At Aunt Duke's house we'd always be up before sunrise. My uncle Emanuel would fix breakfast—eggs, cornbread and syrup—and then I would help him in the garden, weeding and planting. My brother William was soon working for a white family as their yard boy and that meant he wasn't around much; it was up to me to do the chores.

I scrubbed the floors with red brick and lye until the cypress wood was bleached pale blond and I learned to make all kinds of things with my hands. Our mattresses were made of corn shucks and soft gray Spanish moss that hung from the trees. Every summer I gathered baskets of the moss and corn shucks and I ticked them into mattress covers made from bleached cotton cement sacks with heavy twine and a long needle. I learned how to cut up sugar cane stalks and palm fronds and weave them into split-bottom cane chairs.

To get firewood for our kitchen stove I'd take a wheelbarrow and an ax and go down along the river levee or into the swamps, picking up driftwood and splitting planks off old barges that were sinking into the mud. I'd use a long pole to fish floating snags and logs out of the river and lay them up on the banks of the levee to dry while I sat there in the sun and watched the steamboats go by.

In New Orleans the Mississippi River is a part of you. We children weren't afraid of its swamps or alligators or blue runner snakes. The Mississippi makes New Orleans a magic city. There are times when I think back about growing up there and it moves me so much I could cry.

When you passed the age of seven, you became a mother to the younger ones. My youngest aunt, Bessie, was only twelve when I went to live with them, but she took me along with her to the white folks' house to work at little odd jobs and keep out of trouble. We would go over there after breakfast and help get the white children dressed for school and do up the dishes before we went to school ourselves. In the afternoon we would go back to help out again. They paid us two dollars a week.

Between our house and the river there were the tracks of the Belt Railroad, which hauled the freight from the docks up and down the river front. One of the trainmen—a white man called Hot Lips—used to let us hitch rides on his caboose to the sugar cane factories so we could get the big juicy stalks to chew on. We'd take baskets down to the railroad and pick up lumps of coal from the tracks and behind the engine tender. By the time the cold winter days came, we'd have a ton or more of coal in the bin.

Growing up, I knew that some of the children I played with were white and I was colored but it made no difference. In my day Negro and white children rode together on the merry-go-round in Audubon Park. White and black lived next door to each other in our neighborhood and no issue was made of it.

As a little girl, I used to play with a lot of Italian children and when we had a spat, when those boys meddled with me, I hit them right back good and hard. One day when I was walking home from school, a gang of those Italian boys jumped down on me from a tree. I got loose and kicked two of them until they ran, and choked another until his eyes bugged and popped, and caught the last one the next day with a stick and fixed him, too. But there were no hard feelings on their part and I didn't feel they were picking on me because I was colored.

Later on, when my aunt Bessie took me along with her to the home of the Ryders, the white family for whom she worked, I never felt a strong difference either. The Ryders were always lovely to me and gave my aunt clothes for all of us. The best clothes I ever had when I was growing up came from the Ryders, and I was glad and grateful to have them.

Another thing we always got from the Ryders was "the pan." In those days it was the custom in New Orleans for the white families to share their extra food with their colored servants. What wasn't served up at the dinner table was put aside in a big pan for maids or cook to take home to their children. I don't mean plate-scrapings; those went to garbage. I mean if there was a casserole or a roast or bowl of vegetables, it was put aside and after dinner was over and the dishes were done, home it went to the colored house in "the pan."

The pan helped many a Negro widow woman bring up her children. It meant the most in the house with many mouths to feed. But it also was a treat in any New Orleans Negro home because in New Orleans good things to eat are an important part of your life. One of the reasons for this

24

must be the influence of the French Creole cooking, but the other reason is that down there it has always been that cooking and sitting down to a big table of eats was a simple pleasure that was within the Negro's reach.

In his own house the Negro could sit down to the table without fear of someone telling him he wasn't wanted or being asked to jump up and run an errand for a white man. The Negro's wife is usually a good cook—so good that she's cooking for the white man's family, too. And in New Orleans, what with the river and the tropical fruits and Louisiana farm country outside the city, all kinds of real good food have always been cheap.

In my time you could always go out on the river and catch buckets of fish and crabs and shrimp. In our little gardens we grew okra, green beans, red beans, tomatoes, pumpkins, peas, corn and mustard greens. We kept chickens and goats. We had the markets where you could buy any piece of the pig from his head to his tail and fish from the ocean as well as the river.

From the swamps we got soup turtles and baby alligators and from the woods we got raccoon, rabbit and possum. From the trees we picked peaches, figs, bananas, pecan nuts and oranges.

I was brought up to believe that good food was important for the strength it gave you and it was a matter of pride to prepare it properly. I remember just the way the kitchen was in Aunt Duke's house, and all those things we cooked on that wood stove are still vivid in my memory. I remember the red beans with the salt pork and the green beans with the pig tails. I remember how I learned to bake all the hot breads—corn bread, butter cake, biscuits and spoonbread. I can call back the memories of the Sunday dinner tables with the bowls of sliced tomatoes and potato salads and roast pork with yams and gravy.

Even today, being a Louisiana woman, I can't go for this

fancy stuff with the sauce on the poached eggs. The best thing for me after some hard singing is some good old "down home" food—ham and biscuits, bacon and beans and rice and shrimp gumbo real New Orleans style—things like that. No matter how great or rich or high-class a southern Negro of my generation gets, he is still apt to feel the same way.

I recall that not long ago I invited a lot of folks around to my house in Chicago for a Christmas dinner. While everybody was in the living room laughing and talking, I was out in my kitchen helping to get ready a great big turkey with all the trimmings when suddenly it came to me that I had been out on the concert road in the North for so long that my mouth was watering for a little southern cooking.

On the sly, I fixed myself some hot-water corn bread, mustard greens and chitlins. Pretty soon the sweet smells of what I was cooking drifted out of the kitchen and the next thing I knew folks were poking their heads in the door saying, "Hey, Mahalia, what's that you're cooking on the back of the stove? That sure doesn't smell like turkey!"

Before I could stop them, they were eating up all my corn bread and greens and chitlins without waiting for the fancy dinner!

Hot-water corn bread is made with water, corn meal and a little grease. You fry it and eat it with greens and beans. It's the bread that gave the Negroes down South in the old days the strength to work. It stuck to their ribs. When they were so poor that they couldn't get anything to eat but corn meal, God's pure water and the plants that grew in the ground, it kept them going. That's what the old Negro down South grew up on. That's what he cut cotton on—beans, corn bread, greens and a little syrup.

Chitlins are nothing more than hog guts, but when they're cooked right they can be the sweetest part of the hog. The Chicago stockyards used to throw away hogs' chitlins until

26

the Negroes came up from the South and showed them how to cook them.

You buy chitlins by the ten-pound bucket. First, you scrape them under water. Then you boil them and add all that high seasoning—garlic, onion, bell pepper and parsley—right in the pot and let it all cook for about two hours until it makes its own gravy. Then serve it with a side dish of greens or potato salad and you'll lick your fingers over it, it's that good.

When I was a little girl growing up in New Orleans we often had baby alligator for breakfast. When you saw one sunning himself in the swamp or on the riverbank, you'd get a stick and creep up real quiet until you got close enough to crack him on the head so hard he never knew what it was that hit him. You ate the tail baked like smothered chicken with onions and garlic and herbs.

Sometimes we had head cheese—made with the whole head of a hog, stewed on the back of the stove in a big iron kettle until the juice turned to a clear jelly and you poured it into a mold and chilled it. On winter mornings we children would drink orange tea. We'd save the peelings from the oranges and dry them in the sun and then put them in a bag and crumble them up to a powder. All you needed was a teaspoonful in a cup of hot water with sugar syrup for sweetening to make a strong hot drink.

On Christmas we had the most wonderful meals of all. That was when Aunt Duke took over the kitchen. She never let me or anybody else do the cooking on that day and she usually started two or three days before. She would have roast goose and roast pork and plates and plates of vegetables and maybe a whole big raccoon stuffed with sweet potatoes, and she'd be up all night baking hot breads and pies and spice cakes.

That was one day she would serve wine, too. Even in a

Baptist home it wasn't considered a sin to have wine on the table for Christmas, and after church it was the custom to visit around the neighborhood and be served wine and sweet cakes and little cups of chicory coffee that was strong enough to kill Goliath.

The memory of those times is sweet to me and it's the reason that today I'm still happiest when I'm cooking for a big crowd of people in my own home. A good meal seems to bring a warm feeling of harmony among people. You begin eating and laughing and time goes by and soon you realize that you've had a pleasant time together and the day seems bright to you all.

2
Somewhere listening

I say this out of my heart—a song must do something for me as well as for the people that hear it. I can't sing a song that doesn't have a message. If it doesn't have the strength it can't lift you. I just can't seem to get the sense of it.

It's been that way ever since I started singing and I guess I was singing almost as soon as I was walking and talking. I always had a big voice, even as a small child, and I was raised with music all around me.

New Orleans was full of music when I was born and all the time I was growing up there. It was the time when they had all the brass bands. There was still music on the showboats on the Mississippi River and there were all the cabarets and cafes where musicians like Jelly Roll Morton and King Oliver were playing. Ragtime music and jazz and the blues were being played all over.

Everybody was buying phonographs—the kind you wound up on the side by hand—just the way people have television sets today—and everybody had records of all the Negro blues singers—Bessie Smith . . . Ma Rainey . . . Mamie Smith . . . all the rest.

The famous white singers like Caruso—you might hear them when you went by a white folks' house, but in a colored house you heard blues. You couldn't help but hear blues—all through the thin partitions of the houses—through the open windows—up and down the street in the colored neighborhoods—everybody played it real loud.

I saw lots of the famous New Orleans brass bands when I was growing up. They advertised the fish fries and the house-rent parties and played for the secret order lodge dances and funerals. When there was going to be a big fish fry or lodge dance they would fill a wagon up with a load of hay or they'd put some chairs in it. The brass band—some of them were five pieces—would climb up in that wagon and they would drive around town, stopping and playing at every street corner to drum up a crowd.

Everybody who possibly could would go that night to the fry or the lodge party. They would put sawdust down in the yard and string up lots of those pretty-colored Japanese lanterns and have eats on the inside and dancing on the outside. Those parties were the only social diversion Negroes had except for the church. No decent Negro—no church-going Negro, at least—would be caught dead down in Storyville where all the saloons and sportin' houses used to be.

They had the brass bands for the funerals—when a very popular man or a secret lodge man or a sportin' man died. They never had a band behind a minister or an unimportant man.

But people today are mixed up about the brass bands. They didn't play jazz at the funerals. The band would play as solemn as a choir or a big pipe organ—right out in front of the church where the funeral service was being held. Then they would march behind the hearse—all the way to the cemetery. They didn't play jazz on the way either—that's the bunk. After the family had left and the man was buried, then on the way back they would jazz it up. The musicians had been paid so they would play coming back from the cemetery, full of spirit—blow it out free of charge—and the folks along the way would have a good time. That's the way a funeral band really was.

I liked it and approved it. The Scripture says: "Rejoice at the outgoing." So why not have bands for funerals?

The only day I hated to hear the bands in New Orleans was Carnival Day during Mardi Gras when they had the Zulu Parade down St. Charles Avenue. To me Carnival Day was the devil's day, and it's one holiday in New Orleans I will never go back to see. There was too much killing. It was a day of revenge and you'd read the next day in the papers about the deaths.

All week downtown during Mardi Gras the whites had their parades with floats down Canal Street and fireworks and costume balls. Then on Carnival Day, both white and black people put on the masks. Enemies would meet and knife each other. Colored members of Indian clubs like the Blackhawks, the Yellow Pocahontas and the Red, White and Blue Tribe used to "Wa-Wa" against each other, stabbing and slashing. They made the whole city a battleground. One day I was caught between two tribes who were raiding a grocery store with a billiard parlor in the back. I had to crawl on my hands and knees through the yelling, fighting, drunken men and it gave me a horror that has stayed with me to this day.

A day I did like was All Saints' Day. Thousands of New Orleans people went to the cemeteries to put flowers on the graves of loved ones who had passed on, and spend the day singing songs and picnicking on the grass.

Aunt Duke stood for so little play at home that I used to spend all my spare time at the Baptist church. If you helped scrub it out, they might let you help ring the big bell for the early-morning service. On Saturday nights they showed silent movies in the church community hall. There were services there every evening and in those days people thought as much of the evening prayer service as they did of the Sunday service so there was always lots going on for children to watch. Sinners who sat in the back would come forward to be prayed over by the preacher and be saved. On Baptism Sundays the women, all dressed in white, would lead the way out the door and across the street to the levee singing "Let's Go Down to the River Jordan," and the preacher would hold the services right down in the Mississippi, blessing the water and baptizing the congregation.

In those days, once you were baptized, you were looked after properly by the church. You were under the eye of the missionaries of the church, who kept track of whether you attended church and prayer meeting and led a Christian life. The churches of today have gotten away from this. They accept you on your word that you believe in the Lord and they don't see you again until the next Sunday. Today they are not doing the job they should to help people keep the faith. There's bad in all of us and most of us can't save ourselves without help.

I loved best to sing in the congregation of our church—the Mount Moriah Baptist Church. All around me I could hear the foot-tapping and hand-clapping. That gave me bounce. I liked it much better than being up in the choir singing the anthem. I liked to sing the songs which testify to the glory of the Lord—those anthems are too dead and cold for me. As David said in the Bible—"Make a joyous noise unto the Lord!"—that's me.

I know now that a great influence in my life was the Sanctified or Holiness Churches we had in the South. I was always a Baptist, but there was a Sanctified Church right next door to our house in New Orleans.

Those people had no choir and no organ. They used the drum, the cymbal, the tambourine, and the steel triangle. Everybody in there sang and they clapped and stomped their feet and sang with their whole bodies. They had a beat, a powerful beat, a rhythm we held on to from slavery days, and their music was so strong and expressive it used to bring the tears to my eyes.

I believe the blues and jazz and even the rock and roll stuff got their beat from the Sanctified Church. We Baptists sang sweet, and we had the long and short meter on beautiful songs like "Amazing Grace, How Sweet It Sounds," but when those Holiness people tore into "I'm So Glad Jesus Lifted Me Up!" they came out with real jubilation.

First you've got to get the rhythm until, through the music, you have the freedom to interpret it. Perhaps that's why white folks just never do clap in time with my music the right way. I tell them, "Honey, I know you're enjoying yourself but please don't clap along with me."

Besides the church and my aunt Duke, another powerful influence in my life in New Orleans was my cousin Fred. He was my aunt Duke's only son, already a big boy when I came to live with them and by the time I was twelve, he was a grown man.

Fred was the only one who could get around Aunt Duke. He laughed at her scolding and went his way, and she couldn't do anything about it but love him. He was a great big, jet-black, good-looking man with pearly teeth. His nose was built high. He kept his hair close-cropped in fine waves and when he went out on the town, he wore beautiful clothes. We all called him "Chafalaye" after the river in the country near where he'd been born. I was crazy about him and I was always excited about the life he led.

Fred worked hard around the docks and on the river, but he loved the high life of New Orleans. He was no saint and he was a man about town with the other young colored men and all the girls. He got along with the gambling men and music men and he knew the sporting life downtown. He loved music and he bought all the blues and jazz records he could.

I'm happiest when I'm cooking for a big group. *Myron Davis*

Aunt Duke never knew it, but when she was away cooking at the white folks' house I played Fred's records all day long—especially the blues songs of Bessie Smith. Bessie was my favorite, but I never let people know I listened to her. Mamie Smith, the other famous blues singer, had a prettier voice, but Bessie's had more soul in it. She dug right down and kept it in you. Her music haunted you even when she stopped singing.

I don't sing the blues myself—not since those days when I was a child. I don't ever take any nightclub engagements. But you've got to know what the blues meant to us then to understand properly about them. The Negroes all over the South kept those blues playing to give us relief from our burdens and to give us courage to go on and maybe get away.

I remember when I used to listen to Bessie Smith sing "I Hate to See That Evening Sun Go Down," I'd fix my mouth and try to make my tones come out just like hers. And I'd whisper to myself that someday the sun was going to shine down on me way up North in Chicago or Kansas City or one of those other faraway places that my cousin Fred and the other Negroes that roamed away from New Orleans always talked about.

Fred was the temptation side of New Orleans that was outside the church. He and his friends had the independent spirit for fun and living that millionaires spend so much to try to find.

As I began to grow up I felt the same restlessness in me. I was strong in mind and body and I wanted to do something with myself. The music of the blues pulled at me and if I could have broken away from Aunt Duke, the way Fred could as a boy and man, I would have gone, too. But Aunt Duke never let up on me. She held me down.

I know today that I have lived a different life because of Aunt Duke. I know that from her upbringing I got that strong will to survive. When I went up to Chicago, I met a mean world and her training gave me the strength to stand up to it.

Down the street from our house was the Pride of Carleton dance hall. They had jazz music there for lodge dances every Saturday night. The children in the neighborhood were allowed to go and dance from eight until nine while the band was warming up and the people coming in. I was always dying to go but Aunt Duke never let me near that hall. "You sit on your own front steps and listen to that mess if you want to," she'd tell me. "But then you come inside and get into bed."

And on Sunday afternoon when the other children were playing on the levee and the young girls and boys were walking hand in hand, I was always marched down the railroad track to where one of Aunt Duke's church-lady societies was holding a meeting. It was up to me as a child getting an education in school to take the secretarial notes.

My aunt Duke belonged to nearly every colored women's society in New Orleans and she always saw to it that I was appointed secretary so that she'd know everybody's business. She was a power in them all. If she'd been educated, she might have run for mayor of the town and come close to being elected. I would sit there and simmer and make notes while the old ladies made their motions and speeches and I would swear to myself I was going to get away—someway I was going to get away!

I went as far as the eighth grade in McDonough School Number 24 and then I hired out as a laundress to earn some money of my own. I worked ten hours a day and I got to be a real good laundress. I could iron a man's shirt in three minutes and I was good at all those embroidered napkins and linen things.

All the time I was trying to decide what I should do with myself. Down South the two most inspiring kinds of people

I knew—the most a colored girl could hope to get to be—were schoolteachers and nurses. The only other life you could go into was my cousin Fred's world of music and entertainment. I could have gone into that world as a young singer, but it was full of wildness and things I'd been taught to believe were wrong and it frightened me.

It was about this time that the news came from Kansas City about Fred. I was asleep one night when I awoke and heard Aunt Duke crying and walking the floor—the only time I ever heard her cry. And in her hand was a telegram from Kansas City saying that "Chafalaye" was dead.

To this day the family doesn't seem to know how he died. If anybody ever found out, it was lost to us. Whether it was an accident or something that happened in the life he led, I don't know.

I'd been too young to feel the sorrow of my mother's death, but I felt the world swallow me up when I heard that Fred was gone. To this day I still can call back all that happened. They brought him back to be buried at our little church and the crowd that turned out for the funeral was a sight to see.

"Chafalaye" was no saint; but he was loved by all sorts of different people and there was every kind of man and girl there that day. The wake went on all night long and lodge bands formed outside the church and played until I thought my heart would break.

After the funeral was over, the bands began to blow it out without charge. People from everywhere formed "the second line," and they paraded back to the Sixteenth Ward— all the men who'd been Fred's lodge brothers and the men and women who had known him—and took all the saloons apart in one big spree. Everybody said Fred would have loved it if he'd been there, and it would have suited him just right to be buried that way.

38

3
One step toward the Lord

After Fred was gone, I knew the time had come for me to go, too. While I'd been growing up some of the colored people had begun drifting away from New Orleans. Many of the young colored men began to go on from their river boat jobs to become chefs and waiters and Pullman car porters on the big express trains. They rolled out across the United States and the trains carried them away from New Orleans and the Mississippi forever. Today their grandchildren are living in states from Connecticut to California.

My uncle Porter was one of those who advanced himself this way. He had moved on up to a job as a headwaiter in a first-class boardinghouse in New Orleans, where he managed a dining room that seated sixty people. Then he decided to take to the railroads.

In those days the great trains that ran across the country were in their glory. The steamboats were on their way out, but the railroads were the wonder of the country. They had sleeping cars and fancy dining cars and they streaked out of New Orleans to the north and to the east and to the west.

Uncle Porter would chuckle when he told about the first time he found himself flying down the track in one of those express train dining car kitchens with the soup kettles jumping and the whole car pitching and swinging. He grabbed the dining car steward and told him, "I can't stand this! I'm getting off at the next stop and going back to the river, where I belong." But the steward talked him out of it and later on there wasn't a man in that dining car that could touch him when it came to feeding people on a speeding train. They called him "Coal Oil Johnny"—the fastest second cook on the line.

Uncle Porter used to tell me how he would feed four hundred people a day in that dining car as his train ran west across the prairies and the desert to California. He rode the Southern Pacific's Sunset Limited out of New Orleans and the Chesapeake and Ohio's George Washington Express from Cincinnati to Washington, D.C. Later on he rode the Bluebird Special from St. Louis to New York and the Royal Palm from Cincinnati to Jacksonville, Florida.

Young colored men like my uncle Porter took a mighty pride in their food and their service. They wore starched white jackets and they polished the brass floors in those railroad car kitchens with acid until they shone so it was like walking on gold. They leaned out the windows of those big crack trains and saw the whole United States go by. They learned about the country and they banded together in a great workingmen's union that came to be known as The International Brotherhood of Sleeping Car Porters. A. Philip Randolph, one of the famous leaders of the NAACP, rode the trains on his way up to become president of the union.

Today many of the country's Negro doctors and lawyers are the sons of the Pullman porters and waiters who raised their families and put them through college by riding the railroad. Now those days have almost passed. The airplanes and buses are stealing more people away from the railroads every year. Now they've started letting colored folks into the dining cars to sit down and eat a meal, but the age of the railroads is almost over and today there's no pride in good service and the food costs so much you can hardly swallow it.

Other colored people had started going up from New Orleans to Chicago. Some of them came back and told us how Negroes lived better up there—how they rode in buses and trolleys with white people and even had their own automobiles.

My uncle Emanuel went up to Chicago. He worked there for a while as a bricklayer and he made enough money to pay for all of us back home, too. When he came home to visit, he told us how a colored person could go shopping in white people's stores and how a Negro woman could try on a dress and mix with white people.

As children we used to sit and listen to him tell those stories. For a long time we could hardly believe it was true that colored people could live that way. It had never occurred to us that there was any other way than it was in New Orleans and we'd always accepted it—we never even thought much about it. Finally, now that I was growing up and filling up more every day with restlessness, I began to have this longing to go up to Chicago and see for myself.

First my papa went up and took a look, but he didn't like it in Chicago. He kept hearing all about the gangsters and Al Capone and he was afraid he'd be killed by them. The bigness of the city frightened him, and even with all the blessings it had to offer, he came back to New Orleans.

I was frightened by what they told me, but I thought that perhaps the church would be able to protect me from the gangsters and I was determined to go.

In 1928, when I was just sixteen, I finally went, using money I had saved from being a nursemaid and laundress. My aunt Duke was against it. She said I was going to a sinful place and tried to stop me. But I was almost a young woman, tall and strong as an ox with a will of my own, and I told her I had to go whether she liked it or not.

41

My aunt Hannah, who was going back to Chicago, took me along with her on Big Number Four—the express train that ran straight through up North. Before we left we cooked up some food and took it along in a big basket. We sat up in our seats for two nights and a day and ate it. It was many years before I ever saw the inside of a railroad dining car or a Pullman berth. I'd been traveling for years all over the North as well as the South, from New York to San Francisco, before I was able to get a berth to sleep in on a train or to eat in the dining car without being put behind a screen so the white folks wouldn't have to see me.

It was December when we got to Chicago. The wind was blowing snow around and it was so cold my bones were shaking. When we came out of the railroad station I started off walking down the street, but my aunt Hannah hustled me right into a taxi that a white man was driving. Down in New Orleans you'd never go near a white man's taxi, but Aunt Hannah said this was Chicago and the man wouldn't mind driving us. Sure enough, he never said a word about it and seemed glad to have us for his fare.

We drove out to Aunt Hannah's apartment on the South Side of the city where another aunt, my aunt Alice, was living with her children. It was at the corner of Thirtieth and Prairie Avenue in a big brick building with a fancy iron gate and rugs on the stairs that made the place so fancy that I could hardly believe colored people were living in there.

Aunt Alice had a big, clean apartment and she found room for me in one of the rooms with my young cousins. The neighborhood was not far from the stockyards. Lots of colored people worked there and out in the Gary steel mills.

Whenever I think back on those early days in Chicago, I think of what a wonder that South Side was to me—a young Negro girl from a river shanty street in New Orleans. When I came there in 1928, the South Side was the second largest

42

Negro city in the world, second only to New York's Harlem. It started on Eighteenth Street and ran as far south as Fifty-fifth Street. It was squeezed in between the stockyards to the west and the white neighborhoods along the shores of Lake Michigan to the east. It was seven miles long and two miles wide and it held about three hundred thousand Negroes.

The South Side was home to all the Negroes who had come streaming up to Chicago from the Deep South since long before World War I. You didn't meet many colored people from Georgia, the Carolinas and Virginia. Those people mostly went up to New York and Philadelphia and Baltimore and Washington. But you met all the folks who had come up from Louisiana and Mississippi and Arkansas and Kentucky.

Negroes had been coming up to Chicago from those states since before the Civil War, when Chicago was a big stop on the Underground Railway for the runaway slaves who were trying to escape to Canada. In those days, the southern cotton men hated Chicago and called it a "nigger-lovin'" town. And later on, after the Civil War, when the free Negroes kept leaving the South to travel up to Chicago on the Mississippi steamboats and railroad trains, the white southerners swore they wouldn't stay because they wouldn't be able to take the cold weather and the big city jobs. But they were wrong about that just the way they've been wrong about everything else they ever said about the Negro.

The Negroes stayed on in Chicago and they built up their life there until it became the greatest business center for the Negro race in America. Whole townloads of colored people came up North to Chicago and brought their own doctors and ministers and undertakers with them. They lived on the South Side in little clusters of communities that kept growing and expanding toward each other until they joined up. They moved into the white neighborhoods that had held the Ger-

"If We Never Needed the Lord Before" *Columbia Records*

When I cry when I'm singing, I'm not sad like some people think. I look back where I came from and I rejoice. *Columbia Records*

mans, the Poles, the Irish, the Italians and the Jews and all the other people who had come to Chicago as immigrants and struggled to start a new life there.

The white people fought to keep the colored families out. They tried to stop them with bombs and riots, but Negroes kept right on coming. They rented rooms and they bought houses. Later, when the white people gave up and moved away, the Negroes would buy their businesses and the churches and synagogues that the white congregations couldn't take with them.

When I first saw it, getting off the train from New Orleans, the South Side was a Negro city. It had Negro policemen and firemen and schoolteachers. There were Negro doctors and lawyers and aldermen. Here and there you'd still run across a Polish or Italian neighborhood mixed in with the colored, but mostly you could go for miles and miles without seeing a white person. The South Side, like Harlem, was the place the Negro went home to after working to earn his money in other parts of the city. When he got there he could lay down his burden of being a colored person in the white man's world and lead his own life.

The country was still enjoying the fat years of the 1920s, and in Chicago the colored world was in full bloom. Never before had Negroes lived so well or had so much money to spend. I'll never forget what a joy it was to see them driving up and down Southern Parkway and Michigan Boulevard in big, shiny touring cars and strolling in the evening, laughing and talking and calling out happily to each other. The men wore cream-colored spats and derbies and carried walking sticks. Their women had fur coats and led little dogs on leashes. Many of the houses on Michigan Avenue were mansions and the people that lived there had diamonds and silks and drove Rolls-Royces. They could easily afford them because some Negroes had become millionaires in the real estate and insurance businesses.

46

The church was the core of the Negro social life in those days, even more so than it is now, and thousands of us went to church two or three times a day on Sunday and just as often during the week. You had to get in line an hour ahead of time at the big churches if you wanted to be seated for the Sunday service, and the people arriving in big limousines would make your eyes pop.

Where I lived with my aunts, and all along Prairie and Indiana Avenues, Negroes were buying houses and fixing them up really nice. They were planting flowers and shrubs and putting up awnings on their balconies and terraces, and talking about the good times and spending their money.

Chicago still had all the jazz musicians that had come up from New Orleans and Memphis and St. Louis; they hadn't moved on yet to New York City. There were black and tan music halls and cabarets. White people used to come out in crowds to the South Side to hear Louis Armstrong and Earl "Father" Hines at the Grand Terrace Ballroom. At the Royal Gardens and Grande Theater there was vaudeville every night with star performers like Ethel Waters and the Mills Brothers and the Whitman Sisters. I stood in line to hear Bessie Smith at the Avenue Theater and sat in my seat so thrilled to hear her as she filled the whole place with her voice that I never went home until they put us out and closed up for the night.

Going to the Avenue was a real treat for me. It was exciting to see Negroes living so well—my own family had been up from New Orleans for such a short time that we didn't have much money. My aunt Hannah and my aunt Alice were both cooks over in white homes on the North Side of Chicago. Before I could get started with my nursing studies, Aunt Hannah came down with asthma and heart trouble and the doctor put her to bed. That left only Aunt Alice to support the family, and it was up to me to pitch in. Instead of wearing a nurse's uniform, I found myself back doing the same laundry work I'd been doing in New Orleans. Maids and washerwomen were on the bottom, but that was all I knew how to do.

In our apartment, my little cousin Nathaniel slept on a couch in the dining room. Little Alice, who was only nine years old, slept in with her mother. Aunt Hannah had a couch in the living room and I had a couch on the sunporch. In that way, my aunts could cut the rent a bit by letting out one of the bedrooms to a boarder, and we always had a railroad dining car waiter living in one of those bedrooms when he wasn't away on train trips to New York.

Every morning except Sunday I'd be up before six o'clock so I could ride with my aunt Alice on the elevated train to the North Side. I can still remember the darkness and cold of those days. The winter wind in Chicago just takes your breath away and, while I was saving up to buy a warm coat, all I had to cut that wind was sweatshirts and sweaters. Shivering in that elevated train, watching the snow blow and swirl in the streetlights and the sun just starting to come up— those were the days when I was low and lonely and afraid in Chicago. The cold and the noise seemed to beat on me and the big buildings made me feel as if I'd come to live in a penitentiary. Oftentimes, I wished I could run away back home to New Orleans.

But after I got up to Chicago, I stuck. I didn't go back to New Orleans for fifteen years. And whatever I am today I owe to Chicago, because in Chicago the Negro found the open door.

In Chicago, our people were advancing. Not only were they making money; they were active in clubs and all sorts of organizations. And I don't mean this was just organizations like the NAACP. There were all kinds of civic organizations and social clubs. The people were church people, but they were talking about different things than we ever did down South—things like getting educated and going into

48

business. The Negro was doing more than just singing and praying, and I began to see a new world.

It was after I got to Chicago that I realized for the first time that the southern whites had a chain on the colored people. It reminded me of how they grazed a mule on the levee from a stake—he could eat the grass in a circle all around and no further. When I looked back on it, I realized I was simple-minded about accepting it.

On the South Side you saw so many Negroes who owned a business. The Jewish people still owned the delicatessens and the clothing shops, but there were lots of Negroes who owned barber shops and drug stores and little eating places. If a Negro man had a business—even if it was no more than a ham-hock joint or hole-in-the-wall beauty shop or an undertaking parlor—it was *his*. It gave me inspiration to see these things, and while I was riding the elevated trains and busting the washing suds in the white folks' homes, I sometimes thought about someday having my own business.

My aunt Hannah's being sick meant things had to be quiet around our apartment, and to give us children somewhere to go in the evenings, my aunt Alice took us to her church—the Greater Salem Baptist Church. It was the most wonderful thing that ever happened to me. It started me on the right road in Chicago.

In just a few weeks I met the Reverend Johnson, who had founded the church, and all his family. There were three brothers and a sister, all right around my age, and they all spent most of their spare time in church work. When they heard I liked to sing, they invited me to try out for their choir.

There were fifty people in the choir, but at the first rehearsal that voice of mine got going over all the rest. When the choir leader waved his hand to stop us short, I was ready to die. "Here I go," I thought. "Right out the door!"

But instead he asked me to come down in front and try

a solo. I picked out "Hand Me Down a Silver Trumpet, Gabriel." I was praying hard I'd just get through it, but everybody liked the way I sang it so much that I was a member of the choir from then on.

The Greater Salem Baptist Church became my second home. I got to be real friendly with all the Johnson family, and when I came back from my wash jobs on the North Side on the elevated at night, I would get off at the stop near the church and visit. I went to the church socials and picnics and excursions on the lake steamers. There were church services during the week as well as on Sunday, and soon all these church activities filled my life so that I stopped feeling homesick for New Orleans. I was excited about how bright my life was getting to be and I still hoped that I'd soon be studying to be a nurse and find a road that would take me out of the washtubs forever.

4
Come on, children, let's sing!

When the Depression hit Chicago, the life Negroes had built up for themselves in Chicago fell apart. On the South Side it was as if somebody had pulled a switch and everything had stopped running. Every day another big mill or factory would lay off all its colored help. Suddenly the streets were full of men and women who'd been put out of their jobs. All day long you'd see crowds of them shuffling back and forth and standing on street corners. Banks all over the South Side locked their doors and I'll never forget seeing the long lines of people outside them crying in the streets over their lost savings and falling on their knees and praying.

The Depression was much harder on the city Negroes up North than it was on the Negroes down South because it cost them all the gains they had struggled for. Many of the Negroes in the South didn't feel the Depression too much. Some of them could hardly tell the difference from prosperity. They never had had much for themselves and they still had their little vegetable gardens and their chickens and maybe a pig or two, so they could still get enough to eat.

But in Chicago the Depression made the South Side a place of broken hopes and dreams. It was so sad that it would break your heart to think about it.

51

The big fine cars disappeared from the streets. People's clothes began to look more and more shabby, and families began to pile in together to save rent money.

Most of the mansions over on Michigan Avenue got turned into "kitchenette" apartments with a whole lot of people trying to share the same stoves to cook on. Even then, there were many who got forced out and it was nothing to see hundreds of men sleeping on newspapers in the streets and alleyways every night.

The city parks were full of people living in shanties made out of tin and wood scraps. All over the city people were lining up to eat at bread lines and soup kitchens. If you earned a dollar, you felt guilty about spending it on yourself. I remember one day I earned $1.75 washing clothes and on the way home I had to pass the people standing in one of those bread lines. I fished the money out of my pocket and told those people to follow me. We bought a sack of potatoes and a mess of smoked ribs and some neck meat with that money and took it all back to my place and had one big supper.

The colored people began to fight to stay alive any way they could. Men took their cars and turned them into "jitney buses." They would ride around all day picking up passengers on street corners and charging them ten cents to carry them crosstown or downtown. It wasn't lawful and the police tried to stop it but the jitney buses spread all over the South Side, killing off the regular bus and trolley car business until the companies began to give driver jobs to colored men for the first time to try to stop it.

The "Fresh Air Taxi Company" of the famous Negro radio program *Amos 'n' Andy* was based on the jitneys, and so were lots of other things that happened to colored folks while they were trying every way they could to make a little money.

Negroes got so desperate that they joined any group that

might give them a little strength to defend themselves and keep going. Many became followers of Marcus Garvey, a West Indian man, who founded the United Negro Improvement Association and pledged a fight to give colored people a roof over their heads and a blanket to cover them. They held street-corner meetings at which they told everybody to "Buy Black," meaning to spend their money only at colored stores. They organized parades and they formed flying squads to fight the white landlords who were putting Negro families who couldn't pay the rent out of their homes.

I'd see riots in the streets between the landlord's eviction men and the police and the Garvey squads every day. Whenever a landlord began putting people out, the call would go out and the Garvey young men would come running and grab the furniture and put it right back inside. Everybody in the neighborhood would join in, and there would be fighting with rocks and bottles and clubs. Sometimes mounted policemen and fire engines with their big hoses would have to be called out to stop it.

The Garvey people would shout to the landlord that they would shoot him or burn his own house down if he didn't leave families with women and children alone, and after a while a lot of landlords backed down and began to let people stay where they were until the New Deal began to put people back to work.

There were a lot of things said about Marcus Garvey. They said he was a red and a dangerous crackpot—and maybe he was, but he kept a lot of people from losing their homes in those days when there was no one else to turn to.

There had always been a lot of gambling and bootlegging on the South Side, just like the rest of Chicago during the twenties, but after the Depression got a grip on the city it spread like a fever. Negroes were out of work and had no place to go. Often they had only a few cents of relief money in their pockets. They would wander the streets and use

In 1930 Robert and Prince Johnson and I formed the Johnson Singers. *Robert Johnson*

their pennies to get a place to sit out of the rain or the cold. Everywhere there were cigar stores where they played "African Golf" in the back rooms, and you'd see the men standing outside saying, "Try your wrist in here, mister."

There were "book stores" that never sold a book and "milk wagons" that didn't carry more than a few quarts of milk. Everything was a blind for gambling or for a speakeasy. For a time, it seemed as if working for a gambling place or a bootlegger had become the only way there was of making any money, and respectable colored men and women were losing their pride and doing it. And there were sinful places called "buffet flats" that I only heard whispered about where there was a lot going on besides gambling and drinking with the customers.

This was the time when the policy numbers game got started big in Chicago. Everybody was playing his pennies. If you could "catch policy," as they called picking the winning number, you might win enough to take care of yourself and your friends or your family for weeks.

Many of the young colored people lost their way during Depression times in Chicago. The times were so hard that it broke their spirits. And although I didn't realize it at the time, I know now that the Lord must have had his arms around me in those days and he protected me. God moves in mysterious ways—and in a mysterious way, the Depression became responsible for my whole career in gospel singing.

It came about because at the Greater Salem Baptist Church the Johnson boys had formed a little singing and entertainment group. There were the three brothers, Prince, Robert and Wilbur, a girl named Louise Barry, and myself.

Robert Johnson was only eighteen years old, but he was a spirited young man. He was like Sammy Davis, Jr.—just full of pep and energy all the time. He loved to sing and act. He was good at writing skits and directing them, and he had

56

us putting on little plays for the church socials. One was called *Hellbound;* another was *From Earth to Glory* and another was *The Fatal Wedding.* He would play the husband and I would play the wife and the others would play old folks and young folks. We cut up and had wonderful times and everybody enjoyed watching us.

After a while we also formed a little singing group and Prince Johnson worked out our arrangements on the piano. He had his own style of playing and it seemed to suit us just right. We called ourselves the Johnson Gospel Singers. With Prince at the piano, we had a bounce that made us popular from the start.

We improved on the music and strayed from the score and gave our own way to each song. Looking back, I'd say that Prince really was the first gospel piano player in Chicago and we were really the first Negro gospel group in the city.

At first we only sang for our church people, but then we began to get asked around. People who heard about us would come and invite us to sing at their church and then pass us along to another church in another part of the South Side.

The reason was that all over the South Side churches were struggling desperately to keep their doors open. All during the boom days of the twenties, colored people had been buying white people's churches and synagogues. They bought them with big mortgages, but in those good times there was plenty of money to meet the notes. The Depression had stopped the flow of money and the congregations couldn't meet their mortgages and pay for the coal to heat their churches and the electricity to light them. They passed the plate over and over again at the services, but people had so little that the churches began to try to raise a little bit of extra money with suppers and socials.

Our little group, the Johnson Gospel Singers, was just

what they needed. They would collect a little admission money to pay for the coal and mortgage and give us the rest. Sometimes we got as much as $1.50 each a night.

We sang all over the South Side and then began to get invitations outside the city to colored churches in downstate Illinois and in Indiana. We sang at the Baptist Conventions in St. Louis and Cleveland and got more invitations still. So, as strange as it seems, deep in the Depression and only twenty years old, I had a dollar or two in my pocketbook at the end of the week after I'd given Aunt Alice and Aunt Hannah my share of the food and rent money.

People who heard me sing were always complimenting me on my voice and telling me I should be taking lessons. One night in 1932 when we each had made four dollars singing at a church, my girl friend and I took our money and went around to see Professor DuBois about some singing lessons. Professor DuBois was a great Negro tenor who had a music salon on the South Side. He was a tall, light-skinned Negro who had a very grand way about him. He was very proud of his career as a concert and operatic singer and it didn't take me long to find out that he didn't think much of my way of singing a song.

First off, he had me sing the spiritual "Standing in the Need of Prayer." I had such a rhythm inside of me that I kept picking up the beat and out of the corner of my eye I could see the Professor frowning. He held up his hand. "That's no way to sing that song," he said. "Slow down. Sing it like this."

He clasped his hands together and sang in a real sad and solemn kind of way. I tried again, but his way was too slow and mournful for me. I got going again with my rhythm, but the Professor shrugged his shoulders and broke me off in the middle.

"You try it," he told the girl who had come with me.

My friend had a nice voice and she sang the song sweet and slow just the way the Professor wanted it.

"Now that's singing!" he exclaimed. "You've got a fine voice and great possibilities."

Turning to me, he said, "And you've got to learn to stop hollering. It will take time to build up your voice. The way you sing is not a credit to the Negro race. You've got to learn to sing songs so that white people can understand them."

I felt all mixed up. How could I sing songs for white people to understand when I was colored myself? It didn't seem to make any sense. It was a battle within me to sing a song in a formal way. I felt it was too polished and I didn't feel good about it. I handed over my four dollars to the Professor and left.

"Wasn't he wonderful?" exclaimed my friend as we went down the stairs. "I'm going to take some more lessons as soon as I can."

The numbness in me was wearing off and I felt hurt and angry. "Not me," I snapped back. "I don't want to sing none of his high-class music!"

It was a long time before I had another extra four dollars, but even when I did, I never went back to Professor DuBois's music salon. It turned out to be my one and only singing lesson. I haven't had one since.

5
I'm going to live the life I sing about

Not all the other young people in the Johnson group cared as much about gospel singing as I did, and after a while I was going off to sing more by myself. My singing was getting better and sometimes I earned as much as ten dollars a week singing at funeral parlors and at churches.

Ministers who had heard me sing at the National Baptist Convention would come to me and say, "Won't you come and sing at my church?" There are an awful lot of Negro churches in Chicago. One thing about Negroes in Chicago— they go to church. They're not all leading a Christian life, but they go to church. You don't catch a South Side church empty on Sunday. So I got to be known all over that part of the city.

By the middle of the Depression I was traveling outside Chicago to sing in colored churches all the way from New York to California. I remember I once sang in Buffalo, New York, for a nickel a night. The congregation had punch cards and paid a nickel each evening to hear me and the trio I had with me.

Gospel music in those days of the early 1930s was really taking wing. It was the kind of music colored people had left behind them down South and they liked it because it was just like a letter from home.

60

Jazz sometimes seems like gospel music, but it isn't. Gospel singing is an expression of the way people feel and it's older than jazz or the blues. The Negro had his rhythm and his beat while he was still a slave in the cotton and rice fields long before he had a dime to buy a horn and learn to play jazz.

The nickel-a-night and dime-a-ticket programs of gospel music kept me traveling away from Chicago a lot of the time. The little churches would send for me and then pass me along from one to another. The minister's family would give me a room and something to eat and then we would divide the admission money, part for the church and part for my carfare and pocket money. I had to sit up in trains night after night, but sometimes I made as much as fifty dollars in one week. That was really good in those Depression days and much more than I could make ironing shirts in the white folks' homes on the North Side, or working in a factory.

I had one taste of factory work when I came back from one of my long singing trips and found being away had cost me my regular laundry jobs with white families on the North Side.

"Come around to the place where I work," a girl at the church told me. "The man will give you a job packing dates."

"What do I know about packing dates?" I asked.

"You don't have to know anything," she answered. "You just sit there and the dates come at you and you put them in a box."

After a week in that factory I was ready to have them put *me* in a box! It was in an old brick building over on the West Side of the city. The pay was seven dollars a week. They gave me a blue uniform and sat me down beside a big moving belt. Date boxes came shooting along and you spotted your dates in each box as it went past. You didn't dare stop to sneeze for fear your box would be only half full at the end of the line. Machines were roaring and hand trucks were slamming around and everybody was shouting and talking.

I took one look around me and decided the other date packers didn't look like church girls to me. They all were touchy and snapping at each other and looked ready to scratch and claw. I sat there and kept my eyes plastered on that moving belt until I was nearly cross-eyed and seeing dates in my sleep.

Then one afternoon, as we were changing out of uniforms at the end of the shift in the locker room, two of the girls went for each other. They pulled out long knives and began waving them around and screeching. Everybody went flying out the door before the foreman rushed in just in time to stop them from killing each other.

That was enough for me and dates. I took my pay and never went back. I got a maid's job in a hotel instead. I had thirty-three rooms to clean every day for twelve dollars a week, but it was a relief. I worked in that hotel for two years whenever I wasn't away traveling. Later, I worked as a maid at the Edgewater Beach Hotel, never dreaming that twenty years later they would be giving me a banquet there when I made my debut with my first television program.

I had met Professor A. Dorsey, the great writer of gospel songs—he is to gospel music what W. C. Handy is to the blues—and we used to travel together to the same church meetings and conventions.

A lot of folks don't know that gospel songs have not been handed down like spirituals. Most gospel songs have been composed and written by Negro musicians like Professor Dorsey.

Before he got saved by the Lord and went into the church, Professor Dorsey was a piano player for Ma Rainey, one of the first of the blues singers. His nickname in those days was "Georgia Tom" and everybody who went to the tent shows used to know him for the rocking, syncopated beat he had on his piano.

When he began to write gospel music he still had a happy beat in his songs. They're sung by thousands of people like myself who believe religion is a joy.

There are still some Negro churches that don't have gospel singers or choirs and only sing the old hymns and anthems, but among Baptists and the Methodists and the Sanctified church people you will always hear gospel music.

Professor Dorsey would have copies of his wonderful songs like "Precious Lord" and "Peace in the Valley" along with him when we traveled together and he would sell these for ten cents a piece to the folks who wanted to own them. Sometimes he would sell five thousand copies a day. But I was still what you call a "fish and bread" singer in those days. I was still singing for my supper as well as for the Lord.

The more gospel singing took hold in Chicago and around the country, the more some of the colored ministers objected to it. They were cold to it. They didn't like the hand-clapping and the stomping and they said we were bringing jazz into the church and it wasn't dignified. Once at church one of the preachers got up in the pulpit and spoke out against me.

I got right up, too. I told him I was born to sing gospel music. Nobody had to teach me. I was serving God. I told him I had been reading the Bible every day most of my life and there was a Psalm that said: "Oh, clap your hands, all ye people! Shout unto the Lord with the voice of a trumpet!" If it was undignified, it was what the Bible told me to do.

The European hymns they wanted me to sing are beautiful songs, but they're not Negro music. I believe most Negroes—unless they are trained concert artists or so educated they're self-conscious—don't feel at home singing them. Like

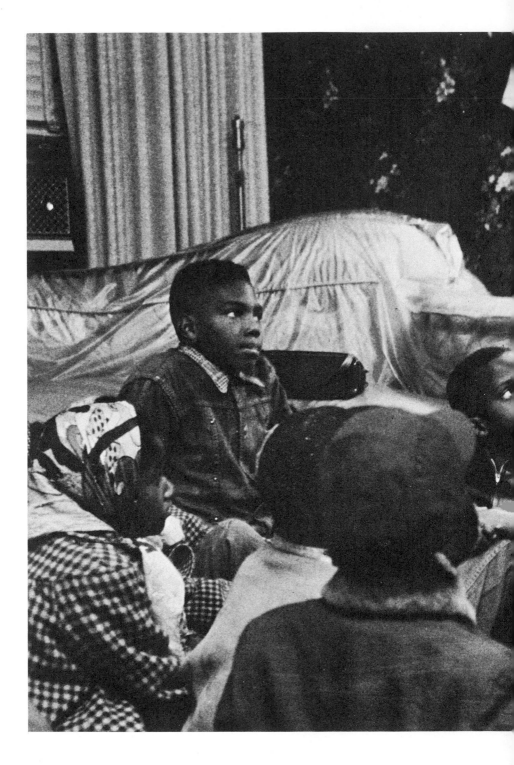

Telling Bible stories to the youngsters in the neighborhood is part of my mission. *Myron Davis*

me, they like to use their hands and their feet. How can you sing of Amazing Grace? How can you sing prayerfully of heaven and earth and all God's wonders without using your hands?

I want my hands . . . my feet . . . my whole body to say all that is in me. I say, "Don't let the devil steal the beat from the Lord! The Lord doesn't like us to act dead. If you feel it, tap your feet a little—dance to the glory of the Lord!"

When I'm singing at concerts, sometimes I whisper . . . sometimes I exclaim and drive the rhythm real hard and sometimes I get right down off the stage on my knees and sing with the folks and keep right on singing afterward in my dressing room before I've said all that I feel inside of me.

Most of the criticism of my songs in the early days came from the high-up society Negroes. There were many who were wealthy, but they did nothing to help me. The first big Negro in Chicago to help me was an undertaker and a politician. His name was Bob Miller. He was the first to present me in a concert in a high school and to raise my admission price from a dime to forty cents. He didn't criticize my simple songs or laugh because I nailed up my own cardboard signs on fences and telephone posts and got in my car and drove around town asking storekeepers to put them in their windows.

In those days the big colored churches didn't want me and they didn't let me in. I had to make it my business to pack the little basement-hall congregations and store-front churches and get their respect that way. When they began to see the crowds I drew, the big churches began to sit up and take notice because even inside the church there are people who are greedy for money.

Another reason I was so strongly drawn to gospel music was that I had a feeling by this time deep down inside me that it was what God wanted me to do. I'd felt closer than ever to God ever since he'd heard my prayers about my

66

grandfather Paul during that long week in the hot summer of 1934.

Grandfather Paul was up visiting with us from New Orleans. We had a big dinner for him with chicken and dumplings and lemonade. I saw him sitting there and having such a good time and I thought how nice it would be for him to have his picture taken before he went down South again. I had a few extra dollars in my pocketbook and I kept after him to take them and go out to a picture studio. Finally he went along with my cousin Alice, but half an hour later Alice was on the telephone. During the picture-taking Grandfather had collapsed with a stroke. Aunt Hannah and I rushed over in a taxi. By the time we got him to the hospital he was barely breathing.

"Is he going to be all right?" we cried to the young doctor in the emergency room.

He just shook his head at us. "I don't know," he said. "I'm afraid he may not even last through the night. You'd better stay close by."

Aunt Hannah was half crazy with fear and grief and she turned it on me. "If you hadn't sent Poppa out into that terrible heat," she sobbed, "this never would have happened. His death is going to be on your shoulders!"

Her words hurt my whole soul. I walked down the hall until I found an empty room and in there alone I fell on my knees and asked God to forgive me for what I had done and begged him to spare my grandfather.

"If you will only let Grandfather live," I prayed, "I will make my life as pure as I can."

I tried to think of something that meant a lot to me that I could sacrifice to show my gratitude. I had never smoked or drank or danced, but I'd always loved going to motion pictures and vaudeville shows. I was crazy about Charlie Chaplin and Norma Shearer and Clara Bow, and the thrill of seeing *The Big Broadcast* with Bing Crosby, Kate Smith,

Connie Boswell, Cab Calloway and the Mills Brothers was still fresh in my mind.

"If you will make Grandfather well," I prayed, "I will never go to another theater again."

For nine days while the doctors worked over my grandfather, I made this same vow to God over and over again. The Lord heard me and suddenly Grandfather began to get better. He walked out of the hospital well and strong and lived on down South for some years afterward.

And since I made God that promise I have never set foot in a picture theater or vaudeville house again. I feel God heard me and wanted me to devote my life to his songs and that is why he suffered my prayers to be answered—so that nothing would distract me from being a gospel singer.

I would not like anyone to misunderstand me. I have many good friends who entertain in the theater. I don't think it's a sin for people to dance and sing and have a good time. I just don't go to the theater because I made my vow to make a sacrifice and I have kept it.

Another thing that gave me the strength to stay with my gospel songs is that all the high life of show business has never had any attraction for me. Maybe it's the Lord's will that makes me that way, but I've never had a longing to spend my time in fancy places or go in for high society.

Even now that life has been good to me and I can afford nice things, I don't own a diamond bracelet and I don't want one. A diamond crucifix given to me by Harry Belafonte is the only jewelry I own besides my wedding ring. All I need to be happy when I'm not singing or in church is a clean home to live in and a chance to cook good things to eat in a nice kitchen.

In my home in Chicago the kitchen is the busiest room in the house. From morning until evening it's hardly ever empty. Whenever I'm in town between my singing trips, I like to have some of my close friends or some of my people from New Orleans and St. Louis visiting with me. We spend a lot of time sitting in the kitchen shelling peas and snapping beans and getting things ready for the oven.

I'm happiest when I'm cooking for a big crowd of people in my own home and my only trouble is that almost everybody else in my family, men and women both, like to cook, too, and you can't keep them away from the stove.

My uncle Porter from St. Louis, for instance, who used to be a dining car chef on the Pennsylvania Railroad, is one of the best cooks I know. When he gets loose in my kitchen, he's in his heaven. You can't hold him down.

Everybody has to jump to keep out of his way. The plates start flying and clouds of steam are up around the ceiling and Uncle Porter is carrying on as if he were back riding the St. Louis Bluebird Express and had to get his food out before the train hit the next station. He has so many pots and pans going that he gets the temperature in there up to 100 degrees and he skips around with his hands going drip . . . drip . . . drip all over my kitchen floor until I get so upset I have to run to my bedroom and cry, "Uncle Porter is out there making a hog pit out of my kitchen and there ain't no way to stop him!"

But pretty soon the biscuits and baked ham and the beans and the corn and the salads start coming through the kitchen door and I have to forgive Uncle Porter all over again.

6
Always look up

In Chicago in 1935, during one of the socials at our church, I met a young colored man who was a graduate of Fisk University and Tuskegee Institute. His name was Isaac Hockenhull. He had studied to be a chemist, but things were so bad then because of the Depression that the only job he could get in Chicago was as a mail carrier for the Post Office.

Ike must have been just about the most dignified postman they ever had. He took himself and life very seriously and he had a speaking voice that called for you to listen to him even if he was only telling you to pass the potatoes.

I was twenty-four years old and working as a hotel maid when I wasn't singing in church. For a long time I couldn't believe that this educated man who was ten years older than me really could be interested in a girl who never knew any school after the eighth grade. But Ike was as serious about me as he was about everything else in life. He believed I had a voice that could make me a great concert artist, and he wanted to take me and lead me and show me the way.

We went together for about a year, and then we were married. It was only a little wedding in my aunt Hannah's apartment, and that was where we lived for a while as Ike struggled along trying to make some money and I kept up with my singing and washing and ironing.

A year or so later we managed to scrape together enough for an apartment for ourselves, but the dark times of the Depression dogged Ike so that he could never get ahead. He'd have regular work for a spell and then he'd be laid off again. He was always trying to find some other way of making a little money.

Before the Depression brought everything crashing down, Ike's mother had had a cosmetics business in St. Louis. She made up lotions and creams and put them out under the name of "Madame Walker" and they sold really well. Ike knew the formulas, and from his training as a chemist he knew how to mix the batches of powders and oils. Often we'd stay up all night making up dozens of jars, and Ike would try to find ways of selling them in Chicago while I would pack a suitcaseful to take with me on the road to sell at the gospel meetings.

I was able to sell quite a lot of cosmetics that way, but Ike wasn't happy. For one thing, he objected that my traveling kept us apart too much. Also he didn't like to see me spending all my time singing gospel songs. Ike's life wasn't within the church the way mine was. He loved me, but he didn't love my songs. He was educated and he thought gospel singing wasn't. He still wanted me to be a concert singer. He wanted me to take voice training, and he and I were always fussing about it.

"Why do you want to waste your wonderful voice on that stuff?" he would shout. "It's not art!"

I told him I didn't care whether gospel singing wasn't art. It had something for me. It was a part of me. I loved it and sang it just the way I had heard the folks sing it down South during those great Baptist revival meetings on the Mississippi River when I was a child.

I could have gone into blues singing—Earl "Father" Hines and Louis Armstrong heard about me and wanted me to come and sing with their bands at the Grand Terrace Ballroom—but I never went because I knew that wasn't the life for me either.

People were always pestering me about becoming a blues singer. They'd tell me, "Girl, you could become a great blues singer." I'd answer, "What Negro *couldn't* become a blues singer!"

I'll never give up my gospel songs for the blues. Blues are the songs of despair, but gospel songs are the songs of hope. When you sing them you are delivered of your burden. You have a feeling that there is a cure for what's wrong.

It always gives me joy to sing gospel songs. I get to singing and I feel better right away. When you get through with the blues, you've got nothing to rest on. I tell people that the person who sings only the blues is like someone in a deep pit yelling for help, and I'm simply not in that position.

Even in those days when I was arguing with Ike I somehow knew that what I had to give was in my singing. A lot of times we don't appreciate who we are and what we are. Even education, while it's a wonderful thing, can make a person narrow that way about himself.

Ike's trying to make a popular singer out of me finally came to a climax one time when we were both out of work. He'd been laid off again and I had lost my hotel maid's job because of being away from Chicago. When we sat down at the kitchen table one morning, we had only a few pennies between us.

But Ike did have a clipping from the newspaper. It told about how the Federal theater project which was trying to create employment for show people was casting an all-Negro company of *The Mikado*. They were holding auditions that week in Chicago to select a girl with an outstanding voice for one of the leading roles.

"You can win that audition easily," Ike told me. "You can have that part if you'll just go around to the theater and sing for them."

I pushed the clipping back at him. "It's not for me," I answered. "I don't want to get mixed up with that kind of singing. I want to stay with my gospel music."

Ike got so angry he was pounding on the table until I thought it was going to fall to pieces. He went on about how I was throwing my life away and missing all my opportunities. *The Mikado,* he said, was a show that would take me all over the country. It would give me training and experience that I would never get any other way. Many people would hear about me. I would be on my way.

"You'll never get anywhere running around to those churches hollering your head off with those gospel songs!" he cried. "Don't you understand God gave you a voice and you're not using it to become a great artist?"

"Not using it!" I shouted. "I'm using it for God's work, that's what I'm doing! When I sing, I don't feel like being a great artist. I just sing the way I feel!"

Ike was down to his last argument, but it was the one that counted. "There's no money in the house, Mahalia," he told me. "That theater work will pay you sixty dollars a week. I'm going out to find work. You've got to do the same."

He laid the clipping on the table and left.

Some people smile when I tell them that afternoon was one of the most painful in my whole life. They don't seem to understand that everything inside me was fighting against the kind of singing I would have to do on the stage. I was feeling so oppressed I hardly knew what I was doing when I finally took the streetcar downtown to the Great Northern Theater, where they were holding the auditions.

I walked up to a side door and asked where they were holding the auditions. A white woman on duty there said, "Right upstairs."

Then she looked at me as if she were puzzled. "But where is your music?" she asked. "You have to bring copies of the songs you want to sing."

I've sung all over the country, in gospel tents and Carnegie Hall, and everywhere people love gospel music. *Columbia Records*

I held up a little book of Sunday school songs called *Gospel Pearls.*

"I'll sing something out of this," I said.

The woman glanced at the little book and shook her head.

"Oh, no," she said. "That would never do. They wouldn't want to hear anything out of that. You'd better go and buy some sheet music."

I wandered off around the corner and found a music store and looked around to see what I could find. Finally I came to a copy of the spiritual "Sometimes I Feel Like a Motherless Child." Somebody had gone and arranged it and stuck their name on a big piece of sheet music. I paid the man twenty-five cents for it and walked slowly back to the theater. The audition room upstairs was packed with girls who wanted to sing for the part. Up front were the judges and a man at the piano.

All the girls around me were tense and excited, but I sat there feeling more miserable than ever. Every time another girl in a row behind me had her turn, I would slip back into her seat, hoping I could hold out until they chose somebody else.

It was no use. They were taking people by the alphabet and suddenly one of the judges called out my name.

For a moment I sat frozen in my seat and then somehow I got myself up and walked up to the man at the piano. I handed him my sheet music. He started playing, and I waited for him to hit the introduction the way I was used to hearing the song sung. In a second or two, I realized the sheet music wasn't arranged the same way. I didn't know where in the world he was or when I was supposed to come in. All I could do was just stand there with people looking at me.

The accompanist went on through the song and looked at me with raised eyebrows. He started in again. This time I let him go until I was ready and then I began to sing. No-

76

body could have sung "Sometimes I Feel Like a Motherless Child" the way I did. I didn't have to put it on. I felt lost and deserted. When I got through, you could hear a pin drop. Finally, one of the judges said, "Why didn't you start to sing when the song was played for you the first time?"

"Because I never heard it played that way before," I said.

"That's the way it's written right here on the sheet," said the piano player.

I shrugged. I could have told him that it didn't make any difference to me—I couldn't read music anyway. But I had a feeling it wouldn't save me.

"Never mind," said the same judge. He leaned over to the other men sitting at the table with him. They all began buzzing to each other and looking at me and I knew what their answer was going to be and it made me even more miserable.

I left the theater and wandered around the streets for a while before I took a streetcar back to the apartment. Ike was already home, and he was more excited than I'd ever seen him.

"You won!" he shouted. "They've already telephoned from the theater. You got the part and they want you to start rehearsals right away. Honey, you've made it! It's your lucky day!"

I just nodded my head. "Yeah, I guess so," I said. I went over and sank down into a chair. "What's your luck been?" I asked.

"Me?" said Ike. "Oh, nothing. I got a job, that's all."

I came back to life like a shot.

"You got a job!" I cried. "Then that settles it. Then I don't have to sing in that show. I'm not going to any rehearsal. I'm quitting right now!"

For a moment Ike looked like he might blow right up and burst. Then he found his voice and started in, but he soon saw he couldn't budge me and he gave up. They gave the part in *The Mikado* to another girl, and that was as close as I ever got to show business.

Things were never really the same between Ike and me after that. He knew he could never change me, and although he'd pester me once in a while after that, his heart wasn't in it. We went on together for a while, but we finally came apart over gospel singing.

A man doesn't want his wife running all over the country, even if it's for the Lord—but I couldn't stop doing it. When you have something deep inside of you, when you're torn apart by it, when you've got to express what's inside of you for the world, nothing can stop you—and I guess that's the way it was with me. I gave the other things up for the work I wanted to do.

Another problem in our marriage was that Ike himself also had a special love which meant nothing to me, and that was race tracks. Even though he was an educated man, Ike couldn't stay away from race horses. He started in by making small bets, but then, like everything else he did, he got real serious about it. He began studying race track forms and charts so that he could become an educated bettor. When he was out of work he spent most of his time trying to pick winners.

Eventually he got to be such a good handicapper that they called him "Seeing-Eye Ike." But even when he became such an expert that he could pick long shots and 100-to-1 winners, I didn't like it. I was too far inside the church to approve of gambling even when Ike insisted it was a business. And as Ike said later, "Mahalia got tired of chicken one day and feathers the next."

Once Ike came home from the track with two thousand dollars in cash and gave it to me to hold for him. I was going over to Detroit to sing and I fretted about what to do with all that money. I was afraid to carry it with me and I was afraid to leave it home where Ike could get his hands on it. Finally, I got the idea of rolling up the rug in our bedroom and laying it under there, bill by bill, until the whole floor was covered with tens and twenties.

I went off to Detroit thinking to myself, "Well, it's safe there. He'll never think to look for it under that rug." But when I got back from Detroit, I looked under the rug before I even took off my coat and all that money was gone. Ike had found it and used it all to buy a race horse!

Ike and I finally separated and later I got a divorce. He and I are still friends, and we always will be because I know he had nothing but my best interests at heart.

People sometimes ask me how I feel about being divorced when my life is so close to the church. I answer that it's because I feel that I was meant to give my life to the church that it had to be that way, and I'm not ashamed of it.

7

Movin' on up

By the time the Depression was over in the late thirties I was earning enough from my singing to keep me away from the maid's work and the washtubs, but I still never expected to depend on my songs for a living and I wanted to try to have a career in business. I took what money I had and in my spare time I went to the Scott Institute of Beauty Culture to learn to be a hairdresser.

By 1939 I had saved enough to buy the equipment for a beauty parlor. I called it "Mahalia's Beauty Salon." Lots of customers came in because they knew me through the church and my singing. Before I knew it, I had five girls working for me. I would ride the trains on weekends to sing in churches in St. Louis and Detroit and other cities and then sit up in the day coaches at night to get back to my hairdressing business.

I studied floral design, too, and I opened up a florist shop that I called "Mahalia's House of Flowers." My florist business did really well, too. People were always asking me to sing at funerals, and a lot of them wouldn't buy my flowers unless I promised to sing. They didn't care how the flowers looked, just so I was there to sing.

I was staying with the songs that came out of the swamps and cane fields and from around the railroad tracks. I never dreamed then that they would be carrying me to concert halls all around the world and that I'd have music critics and all kinds of experts writing about me.

Those were the days long before the jazz bands and the nightclub singers began to borrow the beat and the rhythms of southern Negro gospel music and blues singing and turn them into "pop" songs. Negroes have been doing blues songs, like the ones Elvis Presley sings, for the last 150 years, but we appreciate him because he was one of the first white singers to do it. He learned all that music down there in the Deep South from Negro singers like "T-Bone" Walker, "Bee-Bee" King, "Ivory Joe" Hunter, "Muddy Waters" and "Memphis Slim."

Great blues singers like "Ivory Joe" Hunter sold millions of records in the colored world before Elvis Presley came along and before Pat Boone made "Since I Lost My Baby, I Almost Lost My Mind," but in those days they wouldn't play those songs on the white folks' radio stations.

I still scarcely knew a single white person. I never dreamed that some would become my friends or how much some other white people would show me they hated me for being a Negro who became famous, and make fun of my songs.

All kinds of people were asking me to give concerts. I sang in great big gospel tents, in little old rackety-rack store-front churches and in big ballrooms. I had to learn fast about this new world I was moving into. Sometimes I got right up front in the box office, selling tickets and making change and saying, "Good evening, folks. Glad to see you!" to all the people.

One night a newspaperman who was watching me joked, "You'd better watch out, Mahalia. Some photographer is going to take your picture selling tickets to your own concert."

"That's all right, child," I told him. "Let them go ahead and do that. That'll show some of these dishonest promoters I got sense enough to protect my money."

I was only half joking, too. Gospel songs had become so

popular that men who didn't care a thing about the church or religion were moving in to prey on the public and the singers. I had begun to have real trouble with them on the road and some were up to such slick tricks with the cash box that I had to make it a rule not to sing until they handed me the money they had promised me.

One man from Philadelphia—I'll just call him Mr. Brown—came all the way to my home in Chicago to coax me into singing at a concert he was promoting in a stadium. I signed up to sing for him, but when I got to Philadelphia, he had switched dates. "You won't be singing here until tomorrow," he told me. "But I understand there's a big concert in Newark tonight and I think I can arrange for you to sing up there. Everybody's hoping you'll be there."

When I got up to Newark, the first thing I found was that people weren't just *hoping* I'd be there. They'd already been told I was coming and my name was up on billboards all over town.

I paid a call on the Newark promoter, who was another slick one, and asked him how come he was so sure I'd be there.

"Oh, there must have been a slip-up about notifying you," he said. "Mr. Brown told us he was sure you'd be delighted to sing for us."

"I'll tell you what I'd be delighted about," I said. "I'd be delighted if you'd go outside and take my name off the marquee and tell the people who are buying tickets that I'm not singing."

Outside the crowd was pouring past the ticket windows and the Newark man began to squirm. "I can't do that," he told me. "I've made all the financial arrangements with Mr. Brown."

"You can just forget about any deal you made with that crook," I said. "And start making some financial arrangements right now with me, and I mean cash on the line. I'm

82

not about to be subcontracted out by a Philadelphia promoter!"

I settled down into my seat and waited. The Newark man dodged around the office and carried on about his deal with Mr. Brown but it didn't budge me. Inside, the people who had come to hear me were getting restless. Some of them began to stamp their feet and make a fuss and it was easy to see that if I didn't walk out on the platform in a few minutes, Newark might have one less concert hall.

"Now then," I said. "Do I get paid or do I call me a taxi?"

There was a lot of scurrying back and forth with the cash box and then they handed me a roll of bills. I put them down deep in my pocketbook and went out and sang for the people. Then I drove back to Philadelphia.

Mr. Brown still acted as if everything was just fine and I wasn't telling him anything that happened. I just went ahead and sang at his concert. After his concert was over, I went back to his house where my friends and a group of Philadelphia ministers were having a reception for me.

In came Mr. Brown shaking hands all around. When he got to me, he asked if everthing was all right. "Just fine," I said, "so long as you pay me now for singing for your concert."

Mr. Brown cooled right off in a hurry. "I hear that you got paid for singing last night," he said. "I made those arrangements, and before I settle with you I'd like to have my share of the cash they gave you."

"You're not getting any share," I said. "I did the singing both nights and I'm the one that gets paid for it. I'm sitting right here until you pay me off."

Mr. Brown had to run out of the room, he got so excited. In a minute he was back, waving a pistol.

"Get out of here. All of you!" he shouted. "I'll have you all arrested."

I packed up and went down to a hotel where my friends

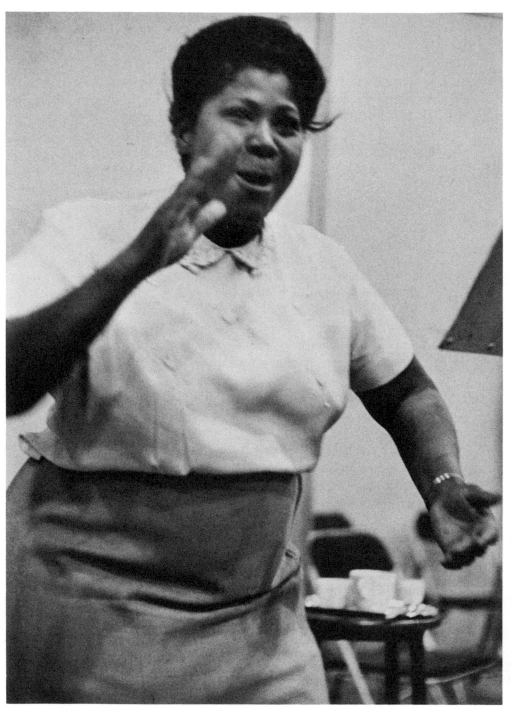

When I sing, I want my whole body to say all that is in me.
Columbia Records

When those professors at Music Inn wanted to hear some gospel music, I just leaned up against the piano and *sang. Warren D. Fowler*

got me a room for the night. Next morning Mr. Brown was banging on my door. When I opened it, I found he had a policeman with him. We all had to go down to court and argue for an hour before I convinced the police that I was entitled to keep the money.

That was the last of that promoter. The way he treated me got the ministers in Philadelphia so angry that they saw to it that their people had nothing more to do with him and his concerts. Mr. Brown went down to the dogs and lost everything.

As for me, I'd learned my lesson. After that I made it a rule to sing only for civic groups and respectable organizations rather than for those gospel promoters who were giving gospel such a bad name.

I had begun to make records of my gospel songs, too. One day in 1946 I was in the recording studio practicing. To limber up my voice I sang just to myself an old spiritual song that I had known since I was a little child:

> One of these mornings I'm going to lay down my cross and get my crown
> As soon as my feet strike Zion, I'm going to lay down my heavy burden
> I'm gonna put on my robes in glory and move on up a little higher . . .

A man from Decca Records named Ink Williams was in the studio and happened to hear me.

"What's that you're singing, Mahalia?" he asked.

"Why it's just an old song we used to call 'Movin' On Up,' Ink," I said.

"But who wrote it?" Ink asked.

"Don't anybody know who wrote it, honey," I said. "I've always sung it, since I was a little child down in New Orleans. I like to sing it my own way."

"You sing it just right," Ink said. "Why don't you make a record of it for us?"

I did and a few weeks later "I Will Move On Up a Little Higher" began to move so fast we couldn't keep track of it. Colored folks were buying it in New York, in Chicago, way out West and all over down South. They've kept on buying it until it's sold close to two million copies.

"Movin' On Up" got to be known as my song. It made me famous, but only with Negroes. I still lived far inside the colored world. Then in 1950 the man who always arranged for my appearances in the colored churches in New York telephoned to tell me that he had heard from a white man named Marshall Stearns who taught music at the New School for Social Research in New York. Stearns spoke to him about a symposium on the origins of jazz music which was going to be held at a place called Music Inn up in the Berkshires in Massachusetts. Music professors from the Juilliard School of Music and a lot of other big places had been invited to come there and discuss and lecture about folk music and jazz.

"What's that got to do with me?" I asked.

"Well, this man Stearns knows all about you and your voice from 'Movin' On Up' and other records and he wanted you to come and sing some gospel songs for them."

"I never expected to be singing for professors," I said. "But if they want me, I'll come, sure enough."

Music Inn, where the symposium was being held, is not far from Tanglewood, where the summer festivals of classical music take place. It's a big old estate that Philip Barber and his wife, Stephanie, bought and fixed up into an inn where people could come to study both jazz and classical music or just to listen to all kinds of music.

When I got up there they were still remodeling the old place. Everybody was running around in all directions carrying ladders and hammers. At night they slept in the cowbarn and the stables and in the ice house. They gave me an old horse stall to sleep in, and I thought to myself, "I finally made it into the white folks' world and look where it landed me!"

After supper Marshall Stearns rounded up music professors and got them into the carriage house, which had been fixed up into a kind of lounge, and asked me to give them a song. I leaned up against the piano and sang "Didn't It Rain, Lord!" and "Jesus, Savior, Pilot Me" and "Movin' On Up."

As soon as I finished, a great big fuss busted loose. Everybody began talking at once. The professors started arguing with each other and asking me all sorts of questions: Where did I learn to sing that way? Who taught me? Where had I learned such tonal shading and rhythm?

After they quieted down a bit, I told them I'd been singing around Baptist churches and gospel tents and at prayer meetings all my life because I loved singing and colored people liked to hear me sing. I told them I'd never had a music lesson. I didn't learn to sing any special way. I just found myself doing it.

Then they began carrying on all over again among themselves and had me sing some more songs and got out tape recorders and played some African bongo music and asked me if it sounded familiar. I told them I didn't know anything about jungle drums, but the beat sounded good; it did something for me.

They argued for a while about that and kept me singing there half the night. When I woke up in my horse stall in the morning, I heard my own voice coming back at me from the carriage house. The professors had already finished breakfast and were playing tape recordings they had made the night before.

"I mean to tell you right now," I said to my accompanist,

88

"we're into something here with these crazy people and I don't know what's going to happen next."

What happened was we stayed on for a whole week while the musicologists and professors and students went around and around with their symposium discussions. They backed me up into a corner and asked me about colored church music and the way some congregations clap their hands and tap their feet. They talked about blues singers, and about the field calls and chants the colored people had made up when they were slaves in the fields of the rice plantations. They kept me singing songs for them and analyzing my style and disputing with me about why I did it just that way until I got all heated up, too.

One young professor kept insisting that I didn't even know my own meter. "You tell us you're singing four-four time," he said, "but I tell you you're not. You're singing twelve-twelve time."

"You're telling me wrong," I shouted. "I stand up here tapping my own foot with a four-four beat and you tell me I'm tapping twelve-twelve. One of us is crazy."

We kept it up all week, but we did a lot of good singing and I moved them with my songs. "Mahalia," Philip Barber told me, "if you'd started out the door and down to the lake while you were singing 'Shall We Gather at the River,' all those experts would have followed you and waded right into the water to be baptized."

8

Keep your hand on the plow

I went back to Chicago and before I knew it everything was happening at once. It was as if a dam had broken. All those music professors must have gone home and started talking to people in the church and concert field. Requests came pouring in from all over. Ed Sullivan invited me to appear on his TV show. I was made the official soloist for the National Baptist Convention, the largest Negro church group in the world. And from New York came an invitation that sent me spinning: would I give a concert at Carnegie Hall?

They said afterward that the music critic of the *New York Times*, who went to Carnegie Hall that night, thought he'd gotten caught in a Cecil B. DeMille mob scene—a Negro mob scene, that is. The crowd around Carnegie Hall was so big that midtown traffic was all tied up. Inside, people swarmed up and down the aisles and up to the top seats in the balconies and boxes. The box office sold out the last standing room and began to put people up on the stage. When it was time for me to start singing, there was just a little place left for me to stand next to the piano.

I stood there, gazing out at the thousands of men and women who had come to hear me—a baby nurse and washer woman—on the stage where great artists like Caruso and

Lily Pons and Marian Anderson had sung, and I was afraid I wouldn't be able to make a sound.

Then I realized that all those colored people had come down from Harlem and some had traveled even from Baltimore and Philadelphia and Boston to be there because I was one of them, and I began to sing with everything that was in me:

> Just as I am but without one plea
> But that thy blood was shed for me.
> Oh Lamb of God, I come to thee . . .

The more I sang the more people in the audience cried out for joy. As the beat picked up, hands started flying and feet started tapping and folks began to shout all over the great hall. Some got up to dance in the aisles with tears streaming down their faces. I got carried away, too, and found myself singing on my knees for them. I had to straighten up and say, "Now we'd best remember we're in Carnegie Hall and if we cut up too much, they might put us out."

But we broke all attendance records that had been set by the Arturo Toscanini and Benny Goodman concerts and the newspaper critics went back to their offices and wrote lovely reviews, so I was a success and a credit to Carnegie Hall and I've been singing there regularly ever since.

After the New York concert, people began telling me that I ought to make a concert tour of Europe. I held back until I began to get personal letters from people in France and Denmark asking me to come and sing for them. In 1952 my record "I Can Put My Trust in Jesus" won an award from the French Academy of Music. Then I said, "If they're going to be nice enough to give me a prize, I ought to be enough of a lady to go over there and say thank you. But I won't be surprised if they don't get my music."

As it turned out, those people didn't surprise me, they

Harry Belafonte is one of the most talented young men I know.
Ebony Magazine

"Silent Night . . ." *Columbia Records*

flabbergasted me. I had thought, "Well, the English at least will understand the words to my songs; I'll probably do my best there." Instead it was just the opposite. The English came to my concerts in Cambridge and in London, but they seemed too inhibited to cut loose or let themselves be carried away; but the French and the Danes, they just made me dizzy.

As a matter of fact, when I got to Paris they had to call out the police to hold back the crowd. The people came around me just the way they did around Louis Armstrong, Big Bill Broonzi and the other big jazz musicians. We went on to Holland, Belgium and Denmark. Even though they couldn't understand the words, those folks were filled with such religious feeling that many wept during my concerts. The morning after my concert in Copenhagen, children filled the hotel lobby with flowers and in the next few days people ordered fifty thousand copies of my record of "Silent Night."

I wanted to sing in Jerusalem at Christmas, but then suddenly the roof fell in on me. All my life I'd been as strong as an ox. Suddenly I was so weak I could scarcely stand. In three months I lost ninety pounds. It got so wherever they laid me down at night, that was where I stayed until it was time to get up for my concert. Sometimes I would have to pray and read the Twenty-seventh Psalm in my dressing room over and over before I found the Lord had given me strength to go out on the stage. When I fainted on the stage one night in France, they canceled the rest of the concert tour and flew me back to Chicago for a major operation.

As I lay in the hospital recovering I thought back to all those white people in Europe who had loved my singing, who made me feel so much at home and so much a part of them, and I thought, "Maybe I have turned a corner. Maybe I'm going to be accepted just for myself and not treated differently because I am a Negro."

It looked as if this was true soon after I came out of the

hospital. In 1954 I was invited to have my own radio program over a big CBS station in Chicago. A year later it became a television show. The critics were wonderful to me. One wrote after the first show: "When Mahalia begins to sing, even the elevator men in the building begin to bounce. The audience wept with "Summertime," rocked with "Joshua Fit the Battle of Jericho" and was so fractured by "Didn't It Rain!" that they had to call an intermission.

Every week I sang for half an hour, by myself and with guest choirs and trios. We sang a lot of gospel songs, but we sang other religious songs, too. I had an Irish sponsor and a Jewish producer and between them they kept after me until I learned to sing Irish and Jewish songs, too. I got to love both kinds, and people wrote in about how much they liked the program so that I got carried away and one day at a meeting at the television station I said, "Why don't we make this a network show instead of a local Chicago program? Then I can sing to a lot more people."

There was a big embarrassed silence. Then one of the TV men said, "We'd love to, Mahalia, but we can't do it. You're all right here in Chicago with a local sponsor, but there isn't a sponsor who sells his product down South that would take a chance on a Negro singer. They're afraid the southerners wouldn't like it."

I just couldn't believe it. More and more white people were coming to my concerts all the time. Even down South they were coming. I knew the same thing had happened to Nat King Cole and how hurt he had been when they told him the white southerners wouldn't stand for a colored man singing love songs on television, but this was even crazier. All I was going to sing was religious music.

"If they're Christians, how in the world can they object to me singing hymns?" I said. "How in the world can they take offense to that? In the name of the Lord, what kind of people could feel that way?"

After Carnegie Hall and the way white people had treated me in France and Denmark and other countries, I'd begun to forget a little what discrimination in the United States was like. It took being back home and traveling again down South to knock the stars out of my eyes.

Until my singing made me famous, I'd lived so far inside the colored people's world that I didn't have to pay attention every day to the way some white people in this country act toward a person with a darker skin. I could go for long stretches and not be made angry or hurt by them. But after I got to be famous, white people began coming to me. They wanted me to sing for them and be on radio and television and in motion pictures. They wanted to be my lawyers, my agents and my business managers.

Whenever I've sung on the TV shows of Steve Allen, Ed Sullivan, Bing Crosby and Dinah Shore, white people in the South as well as the North have written to tell me how much my singing meant to them. It's gotten so I spend part of almost every day with a white person, yet when I come down off that concert stage they're still likely to treat me as if I had leprosy.

I'm no special Negro. I don't want to be treated differently than any other member of my race. It's just that when you move back and forth between the white and colored worlds every day, the stupidity and cruelty of some white people toward the Negro hits you so hard you don't know whether to explode or pray for someone who has such hatred in his soul.

A little while back I made a concert tour through the South from Virginia to Florida. There were lots of white people at those concerts and they sat side by side with colored folks because my instruction to the ushers is to say, "Come right in. Pick a seat and sit right down—anywhere." Because if you come to hear religious music, you're not supposed to feel any bigger than anybody else. Those white people—and a lot of them were ministers—applauded just as hard as anybody in the audience, and afterward some of them came around to tell me how much they had enjoyed the evening.

But the minute I left the concert hall I felt as if I had stepped back into the jungle. My accompanist, Mildred Falls, and I were traveling in my car, a Cadillac. My cousin, John Stevens, a young actor and drama teacher from Chicago, was doing the driving. From Virginia to Florida it was a nightmare. There was no place for us to eat or sleep on the main highways. Restaurants wouldn't serve us. Teen-age white girls who were serving as car hops would come bouncing out to the car and stop dead when they saw we were Negroes, spin around without a word and walk away. Some gasoline stations didn't want to sell us gas and oil. Some told us that no rest rooms were available. The looks of anger at the sight of us colored folks sitting in a nice car were frightening to see.

To turn off the main highway and find a place to eat and sleep in a colored neighborhood meant losing so much time that we finally were driving hundreds of extra miles each day to get to the next city in which I was to sing so that we could get a place to eat and sleep. It got so we were living on bags of fresh fruit during the day and driving half the night and I was so exhausted by the time I was supposed to sing I was almost dizzy.

When the white people came crowding around us after the concerts—ministers, teachers, educated people—I thanked them for their praise but I felt like saying, "How big does a person have to grow down in this part of the country before he's going to stand up and say, 'Let us stop treating other men and women and children with such cruelty just because they are born colored!' "

The hardest thing for colored people to understand about white people is this fear and hatred they seem to have of us.

Ed Sullivan first invited me to appear on his show in 1950. *CBS*

I was really pleased when I got my own TV show in Chicago, but it was a disappointment to find that no one would sponsor a network show because of prejudice in the South. *CBS*

Down South white children spend more time with their colored nursemaids than they do with their own mothers. Many a white child has nursed off a colored breast without his folks ever knowing it. As a nursemaid, I know that. Sometimes it was the only way you could get a baby to quiet down and take his bottle, and even we young teen-age Negro girls did it so that the babies we were caring for would take their bottles.

Since the days of slavery colored men have been working inside white people's homes as pantry men, butlers and chauffeurs, helping bring up the little boys and girls and taking a pride in being a trusted part of the family. Up North today many families rely on Negro maids and baby-sitters. If they trust their most precious possession—their child—to us, how can they have such hate and fear of us?

Actually I don't think the great majority of Negroes want to be spending half as much time with the white man as he worries and frets himself about. The Negro just wants to be able to get into nice places to eat and sleep and be able to buy things at the same stores, have a good home and have the same rights in education.

As far as socializing goes, we colored people have been kept away from the white man's social life so long that we're not missing him. We've got our own social life and family life and it can be rich and satisfying. And I wouldn't be surprised if a lot of the time it's even happier than white folks'!

Negroes make a mistake in believing they're going to be in paradise if they have more money and less discrimination. It will be nice to have the clean homes to live in and education for the children and other opportunities, but for a long time the Negro hasn't needed money to be happy. Colored people are used to being happy with less. In New Orleans they lived freely. They didn't work on Saturday, and Blue Monday nobody worked either. They had dances and house rent parties and socials, and lived slowly.

Here and there you find colored men who marry white, but I think they are going the long way around to find happiness. I have nothing against intermarriage except that it means a Negro man leaving behind the Negro woman who has worked and suffered with him since slavery times.

I say to him, "What is going to happen to the Negro woman if when you're successful you marry out of your race? Who's going to make her feel she's an important lady?"

Ever since slavery times it's been the Negro woman in the South who has had to shoulder the burden of strength and dignity in the colored family. Even when she let the white man have his way with her—and it must have happened often because many, many Negroes in this country are not black like myself—I believe she went with the plantation master or the field overseer or his sons so they would be easier on the colored men on her plantation. She had some control over the white men and could make them act more kindly toward her people.

Down in the South the white man has never given the Negro man a job he could be very proud of. He has always called him "Boy" or by some nickname. It was hard for colored children to be proud of fathers who were treated like that and it was usually the Negro mother who had to keep a certain dignity in the family to offset the inferiority the white man inflicted on her husband. She held her head up high and she showed the way to her children.

I believe that right now down South behind most of those brave colored school children and college students you'll find there still is a Negro mother telling them to hold their heads up—to face the white men who try to hurt them and ridicule them—with patience and dignity. When I hear people talking about Communists being behind the colored students, I have to laugh. It's not Communists—it's Negro mothers who believe it's time for their children to fight for their rights and a good education.

I'm so interested in seeing more young Negroes get educated! Our young people have got a long road to travel to make the most of their new freedom. They must be able to talk well and make sense every inch of the way with the white people. And this again is where the Negro woman still has a great task to help them reach that goal. Now is the time for us to understand how important education has become for our race and to try to hold our younger people together to get them through school the same way the Negro slave woman used to labor to hold her family together as they grew up in plantation times. We must pray and work every day to see to it that the wonderful spirit of this new younger generation of Negroes is not broken.

The Negro woman has helped make the colored world decent and strong. She has stood by and raised the children alone when the hurt and frustration her husband suffered weakened him and drove him to leave his family and become a wanderer. The plain common Negro church woman has always been the backbone of the colored church and has given the last dollar she earned scrubbing floors to the collection plate to keep it going because she knew it was the salvation of her family.

Today fifty percent of Negro business, North and South, is run by Negro women. Negro women have made beauty culture a big business. Negro women like Madame K. C. Walker have cosmetic shops from coast to coast and every Negro community has its hat shops and flower shops and dancing schools for children, run by colored women. So if a colored man wants to marry a woman he can be proud of, there's no need for him to seek out a white woman.

9
Going home

I can't speak for the sophisticated and highly educated Negroes in the North, but I do believe that the great bulk of colored people still prefer to attend their own churches rather than the white churches.

I don't think that most Negroes feel they have to go to a white man's church to learn to serve God. The service of the white man's church is often too rigid and formal for the Negro, who likes to express his feelings in singing and hand-clapping and getting up to testify to the congregation about how the spirit moves in him. Some of the best sermons I've ever heard have been preached by a colored minister who goes on for a couple of hours at a time, jumping up to talk for a while, then sitting down with his congregation and joining in the singing and then getting up to preach some more, until everybody is filled with such rejoicing that you come close to shaking the meat off your bones.

Of course, there are some Negroes who have a taste for hymns and formal services just like there are white people who aren't inhibited or ashamed about showing their religious feelings. I've looked down from the stage too many times when I'm singing to see white men and women moved to weeping not to believe that some can be as emotional as any colored person. I've seen them clap their hands and rejoice with the spirit of loving Jesus. Today, there's a great awakening of emotion in the white man's religion, too. White ministers who come to my concerts tell me what a great feeling it has given them to be able to express their emotions freely. White people call me long distance on the telephone and write me letters, too, to tell me the same thing.

One newspaperman asked me recently, "Why do the white people really come to hear you sing those church songs, Mahalia? What do they really get from it?" And I answered, "Well, honey, maybe they tried drink and they tried psychoanalysis and now they're going to try to rejoice with me a bit. If more white people only dared let themselves go and show their true deep feelings maybe some good might come of it."

So I believe that there should be all kinds of churches to suit everybody, white or colored, for those who like to worship in a quiet way and for those who like to worship with emotion. There's still a lot of us who like to shout and holler in church and don't mind hand-clapping and the preacher hopping and skipping around the pulpit and we'd be glad to have white folks who feel the same way join us.

In fact, I hope to be a part of such a church and religious service myself. For nearly thirty years I've been traveling all over to carry my gospel songs to people. For the last ten years I've averaged two hundred concerts a year. I don't want to be doing just concerts all my life.

If the Lord will let me, I'm going to be an evangelist. I'm planning now to build a big evangelist temple in Chicago and get up a group of fine gospel singers who have the real beat to help me express to people the happiness and strength that can come from the Lord.

I want to make my temple nonsegregated, nondenominational (even though I'm a hard-shell Baptist) and have our services televised nationally—with or without the sponsors that the TV people keep telling me are so afraid of the

South—so that white and colored people all over the country can hear our singing.

I want to have all kinds of classes and groups connected with the temple that will help the many talented young men and women who are still blocked in so many places—young singers, musicians, actors, dancers—to give them another path of study besides commercial show business which has so many sinful temptations and frustrations for young colored people.

I want to prove to young people—to all young people—that they can take what they've got and go to great heights if they believe in themselves. Some of the young colored people with great talent get hurt so badly by discrimination that it breaks their spirit. I see some that are so bitter. Even the ones that break through are still hurt deep inside and ready to fight. They have a shell around them.

When I see the talent that just needs a chance, it saddens my heart. They come to me and say, "Mahalia, please help us . . ." I say, "I'm trying to, honey. I'm going to. Just give me a little time. I just got my toe in the door after thirty years of trying. It takes time to be delivered by the Lord. The Lord took me and I was nothing and He put me up. It can happen to you, too. If the Lord can bring me this far —take me out of the washtubs and off my knees scrubbing other people's floors—then He can do as much and more for others."

I hate to see the commercial world take the songs that have been the strength of the colored people and turn them into jived-up nightclub acts and rock-and-roll records to be laughed at and joked about.

One evening not long ago I was in New York City doing some shopping. As I walked down a street in Greenwich Village where I like to go to look for pieces of ebony statuary, I suddenly heard this singing with a gospel beat.

105

I really believe that most colored people prefer their own churches. *Myron Davis*

I looked in the door of a nightclub and there was a Negro girl with her hair bleached red-blond swinging a gospel song that I had first heard as a little girl in a Holiness Church in New Orleans. The place was packed with white people who were laughing and eating and drinking and hand-clapping. Bartenders were beating out the rhythm of the song on church tambourines and waitresses were even using tambourines as trays to serve drinks!

It was a sight that made me so sad and so sick that I'll never forget it. The dignity of a colored church and of all religion was being debased so that a few people could make some fast money.

When they take gospel singing into nightclubs and put out "pop gospel" records, they are blaspheming against the Holy Ghost. I make two kinds of gospel song records—one for Negroes who like to tap their feet, and one for those who like religious songs sung for them. But I would never sing a song to be laughed at or to help sell a bottle of whiskey!

I've always wished that I could reach both white and colored people on television through a religious program. Network television has seldom given me the right stage setting for what I've felt down in my heart, and they're always running themselves and me crazy because they're so pressed for *Time*.

TV and I don't see eye to eye about time. Time is important to me because I want to sing long enough to leave a message. I'm used to singing in church where they don't stop me until the Lord comes. But the first thing they start telling me when we get to a TV rehearsal is "Look out!— Watch your time!" and they start out to cut the song down.

Dinah Shore, who has been more gracious to me than anybody else in television, pointed it out to me one Easter when I wanted to sing "But Surely He Died on Calvary" on her program. "Mahalia," she said, "for you to sing that song the

108

way you'd like would take about five or six minutes and they wouldn't know what to put on after you finished."

In television there has also always been the trouble with some producers that are trying to change me. I get a feeling they're trying to slick me up and make me into a commercial entertainer. Real gospel singing lifts people up and brings understanding and a strength of religious faith back to those who hear it. It's not supposed to be just an entertainment.

A big orchestra is not for me. I sing better just standing flat-footed with a piano or an organ, but usually when I walk in the door of a television rehearsal studio there sits this big orchestra and I can't escape it.

Even with the orchestra they want to squeeze me in. They will have some comedy or dance routines that take up most of the time. Or they give me a feeling that I'm too sad for the program—that my song is a problem to them.

Some of these producers and directors worried me so much that I got to dread being asked to work with them. Everybody would come running up to me and say, "Oh, Mahalia, I just read where you are going to be on that big television show again! Isn't that thrilling?" and to me it was like going through hell and damnation. Nobody knows the suffering I felt when I got booked into one of those mixed bills that were just vaudeville shows, and I'd find myself standing backstage waiting my turn, listening to all that jazz and folly that was going on the air and wondering how I could come out and lift people up. Nothing but the grace of God could help me sing with any conviction in the middle of all that commotion.

But I've suffered for it because in the long run it has a good effect on people. I'm reminded of the time back in the days in Chicago when I first got to sing on the radio and some of my people on the South Side who should have been in church stood in bars and taverns listening to me sing the gospel. One man wrote to me that he was standing at the bar drinking when I came on the radio and said, "I want you to know that I didn't touch a drop of that beer until you were finished!"

I wrote him back that I noticed he said he quit only until I finished but I was glad of his listening. In the same way, I'd think to myself that it was wonderful that so many people would hear the songs on a TV network—but why did it always have to be in the middle of a vaudeville show?

Then one day the people who were in charge of the Dave Garroway *Wide, Wide World* television program called me up to invite me to appear on a Christmas program. I said I would love to but that I was going back home to New Orleans to spend Christmas with my own people for the first time in thirteen years.

"Why, that's all right," the Garroway man answered. "Couldn't you sing for us from down there?"

"You mean from my own little church?" I asked.

"Sure," he said. "If you can set up the program."

Going down home to New Orleans for that Christmas turned out to be one of the most wonderful times in my life. Before I left Chicago I must have shopped for a month for my family. There were so many new children to buy Christmas presents for and so many aunts and uncles from the city and the country around New Orleans I would be seeing for the first time in many years.

Driving South in the car I could hardly sit still. There was so much to think about—to realize that I was on my way back to be with my own people and going to do a big television show in the tiny, little church where I had first sung in the children's choir when I was only five years old. Never would I have dared that such a dream could come true.

I got to New Orleans about a week before Christmas Eve but for me it was like Christmas for the whole time I was there. The big colored churches in downtown New Orleans

110

had got the news about the Garroway program and the first night I was in town ministers came calling on me inviting us to broadcast from downtown. They had big choirs with trained singers, they told me, and they thought they would be able to present better music than the little old Mount Moriah Baptist Church on Water Street. I thanked them for the invitation but said I preferred to stay right in my own little church where I was raised and received my first religious training.

"We're going to roll up our sleeves," I told them, "and show you people from downtown just how much a little church can do."

The next day I got in my car and began driving around the Sixteenth Ward to see if I could re-form part of the choir that had sung together when we were all children.

Some of my old friends had never left town but before they'd join the choir, I had to convince them that I hadn't changed.

A lot of them didn't have TV sets and they didn't know what kind of singing I'd been doing and what I was like. They saw my big car with the Illinois license plates and hung back from me wondering how far I might have drifted away from them. In the beginning I had to do a lot of talking about the things we used to do together as children to make them realize how important that life had been to me.

We talked about how we played out on the Mississippi River levee and I recalled the songs we used to sing out there as children—"Couldn't Hear Nobody Pray," "High Society," "When the Saints Go Marchin' In" and "I'm Forever Blowing Bubbles"—and all the others we sang for the rhythm and feeling we could give them.

The more I talked the more some of the old friends began to come 'round. They'd smile and say, "Now do you *really* remember that!" and then they'd loosen up to say, "Well, I know you've been traveling all around the world but I bet

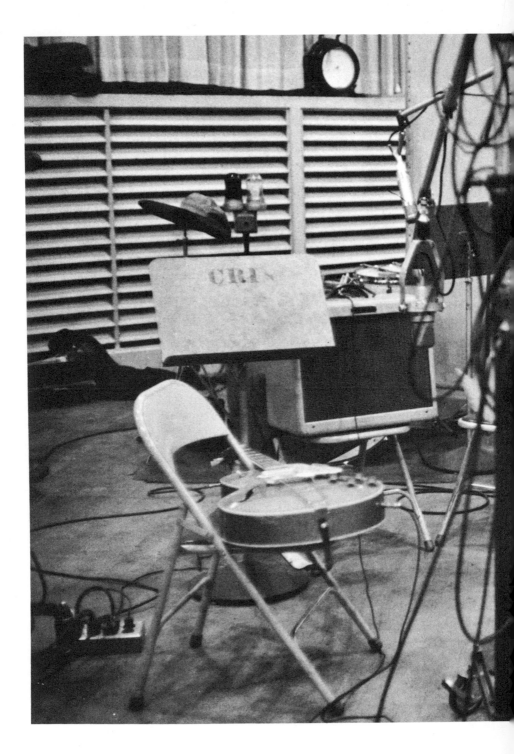

It can be hard singing for records and television, with their orchestras and their time limits. But I keep at it because I think my music can do some good for people. *Columbia Records*

you haven't had any good old Louisiana food in quite a while. You'd better come right on inside and sit down."

At Christmas time the colored people in New Orleans take pride in doing their best cooking of the whole year and the things they served me to eat were enough to make you ache, they were so good.

There were red beans and rice and French bread, toasted and buttered, with great big oysters from the Gulf of Mexico to drop on top. There was seafood—red snapper baked with tomato sauce and Louisiana seasoning, big platters of boiled crabs, sea turtle cooked like smothered chicken and big platters of a vegetable called pepper grass that you eat like turnip greens after it's been cooked with ham or smoked ribs or salt pork.

We would sit together and eat and laugh and talk and I would say, "Child, I haven't had this kind of food in twenty years! It takes me back and I want you to help me come back to the church here. Come out and sing with me on this television program and show the people how we used to do it together."

I wasn't just talking to coax them either. I meant every word of it because to tell you the truth they can still sing down there in those little New Orleans churches. They can beat me singing right now.

They were shy about it at first but then they said they would try it and we got going. Every day we rehearsed our choir. We were going to show just a part of the church's Christmas program on television ("Time" again!) but we worked to get it just right. My own little cousin, Molly, a beautiful little black girl with glossy hair and keen features, played me singing as a child. As I saw my past coming to life I found my mind running back to the days when I had skipped in and out of the church as a little girl. Sitting in the church watching her sing made me tingle all over.

It was warm in New Orleans that year even though it was

114

December, and in the evenings I walked up and down the streets of the neighborhood in which I had been born, looking at places that had been alive only in my memory—where as a little girl like Molly I had watched the boats on the river from China and South America and lain awake at night listening to the Negro stevedores singing and whistling as they worked on the river boats and the belt trains that ran alongside the river to pick up the ship cargoes.

I drove over to see the big changes on Charles Avenue where they were converting some of the great, white pillared mansions into apartment houses and boardinghouses, and recalled how there were said to be twelve millionaires living right on that one avenue when I worked in the white folks' homes where my aunt Duke cooked.

All the decent clothes I had had as a little girl had come from those white peoples' homes and so had a lot of the food that helped us colored children to grow up. Now there was a different spirit in the city. It had put the colored and white races apart, and Aunt Duke told me that there was a meanness among some of the new white people that she had never known. It seemed strange that New Orleans, a city of so much mixed and colored blood, should be carrying on that way, but the bitterness about the new rights the colored people were pressing for was doing it.

The day before Christmas we took all the children downtown and bought more horns and balloons and things (I had a time with those children!) and then after supper we went around to the Mount Moriah church for the Christmas Eve service by the Reverend Robert Hack, who had been just a young Sunday school teacher when I was a little girl; he had married a friend of mine and gone on to become the pastor. My father, who was then still alive, was there with us that night. So was my older brother, Peter, who is gone now, and my sisters Pearl and Yvonne, and of course Aunt Duke and Aunt Bessie, the two aunts who had brought me up.

115

Afterward, Bill Russell, a white Chicago musicologist who moved down to New Orleans so that he could continue his studies of Negro music, came around with a surprise—a Christmas tree—and set it up for me.

We stayed up so late talking on the telephone to wish people Merry Christmas that I slept late on Christmas morning. I woke up and began to worry a bit about the television program. While the children were trying on dresses and opening candy, Bill Russell and I went around to the church. The television men were there with their trucks setting up the special equipment but the neighborhood was very quiet. I thought to myself, "Everybody is home cooking Christmas dinner. Maybe we're not going to have much of a crowd after all."

But then the people began to come. The streets outside began to fill up and the choir singers arrived right on time. Some were a little bothered with stage fright but they weren't going to let me or their church down. We went in and practiced and loosened up and the church filled up to the rafters. I looked out and saw the faces of the people who had sung with me as a child and cried with happiness that I was back with them.

When the red lights on the cameras showed we were on the air we went right to it. I had chosen two of my favorite gospel songs—"Born in Bethlehem," a good song with a driving beat to it, and "Sweet Little Jesus Boy," which is slower but has a powerful, moving feeling to it. And everything went just fine.

We knew we had done just as well as any big church and hadn't gotten scared off even though they told us ten million people were watching.

Afterward, to celebrate, we packed home so many friends and relatives that we had to turn both Aunt Duke's and Aunt Bessie's houses into dining rooms for the Christmas dinner. We started out with Louisiana gumbo and went on

116

to roast turkey with all the extra dishes and finished up with blackberry pie, jelly roll cakes and port wine. While we ate, the long distance telephone calls and telegrams kept pouring in, making each moment more joyous than before. It was one day when my aunt Duke admitted I had come a long way and still managed to stay with the church. She always worried so much about me being in show business.

The next day Christmas was over and I came down to earth fast. I went downtown to do some shopping. Many people, both white and colored, recognized me and came over to tell me how much they had enjoyed our television program. But the weather had turned even warmer and it was so hot I could scarcely breathe. I wanted to get to someplace where I could sit down and have a cold drink, but there was no restaurant nearby that would serve a colored person. Here I was with all the white people calling me up long distance from Texas and California and other far-off places to tell me how much they loved me and my singing and in New Orleans I couldn't even get a cold soda or a taxi ride. (It wasn't until the fall of 1962 that New Orleans restaurants integrated and admitted colored people for the first time in eighty-five years.)

Suddenly I knew I had had my homecoming and it was all over. I could come back down to New Orleans for wonderful visits with my own people, but I couldn't stay. Chicago and the North, where I was used to Negroes being more free, was where I belonged.

10
I been 'buked

Even though it's not anywhere near as bad as the South, my second home, Chicago, gave me a bad time, too, when I set out to buy a home.

For a long time I had a nice apartment in Chicago, but dreamed of having a house all to myself, a little place with trees and grass and a garden. The idea meant especially much to me because my concert tours have forced me to spend so much time in hotel rooms and other people's houses. Also, I've always liked to sing as I cooked and cleaned my apartment and worked around my kitchen late at night and there were plenty of people who objected to it.

I remember when I was just a "fish and bread" gospel singer on the road, I stayed over at my friend Genese Smith's apartment in St. Louis, Missouri. Genese is another gospel singer with a lovely voice and we were sitting in her kitchen late one night singing and humming religious songs when the landlady came tearing upstairs and like to knock down the door hammering on it and shouting at us to go to bed. Poor Genese was so embarrassed she was ready to die but I told her, "Don't let it worry you, honey. I rent, too, and they do the same to me back in my apartment in Chicago. But one of these days I'm gonna own the whole apartment house and I'll be able to holler as loud as I like."

118

I got the apartment house, but it didn't change things. Even though they were my tenants, the people still came flying upstairs to scold me when I sang loud to myself.

At first I looked for a house by myself. I would get into my car and drive out into the suburbs on the South Side of Chicago until I came to a neighborhood that I liked. Then I would watch for "For Sale" signs and stop to inquire in a friendly way about the house.

The attention I was getting every day from white people from my singing had sort of confused me, and it took me some time to understand that they still didn't want me as a neighbor. Every time I asked, they would tell me sorry, the house had just been sold, or that they had changed their minds about selling.

Finally I gave up being friendly and went to a real estate agent. She found a white man—a surgeon in a nice neighborhood—who knew me through my singing. He said, "You tell Mahalia Jackson I'd be proud to sell my house to her."

Well, when the news got around his neighborhood the people nearly went crazy. Everybody was holding meetings up and down the block. A Catholic priest even rallied his parishioners together and told them not to move. You'd have thought the atomic bomb was coming instead of me.

When they found out they couldn't stop the doctor, they went after me. My phone rang at all hours of the night and voices warned, "You move into that house and we'll blow it up with dynamite. You're going to need more than your gospel songs and prayers to save you. Wait and see what we do to you!"

They got me so upset that I prayed to God every night to guide me in the right thing to do. I hadn't intended to start a one-man crusade. I didn't want to go running through people's backyards to white people's houses. All I wanted was a quiet, pretty home to live in. Finally I bought the house.

I was threatened and my house was shot at when I first bought my home in Chicago. *Ebony Magazine*

At first they shot rifle bullets through my windows, and police were posted outside for almost a year. When Ed Murrow asked me to appear on his *Person to Person* program in a telecast from my home, I invited all the children in the neighborhood to come in and be on the program with me and have ice cream and cake. A lot of them came and I thought everything was going to be all right.

But those white folks wouldn't stay there with me as a neighbor. One by one they sold their houses and moved away. And fast as a house came on the market a colored family would buy it.

Today the neighborhood is almost entirely colored—doctors, lawyers, businessmen and their families. The white people swore we would ruin it, that it would be a slum overnight. But it hasn't changed. The grass is still green. The lawns are as neat as ever. Children still whiz up and down on their bikes. On Sunday mornings when I sit in my garden it's so quiet all you hear is the birds singing. The same birds are still in the trees. I guess it didn't occur to them to leave just because we moved in.

It was just about the time that I got my house that I met two young Negroes who were destined to become famous. I had gone out to sing at the Baptist Convention in Denver, Colorado. There, the Reverend Russell Roberts of Atlantic City, New Jersey, introduced me to two clergymen from down South. One was the Reverend Ralph D. Abernathy, who is pastor of the church in Montgomery, Alabama, where the National Baptist Convention was founded. The other was a young preacher fresh out of divinity school serving his first pastorate in a downtown Montgomery church that Negroes have been attending since slavery times. His name was Martin Luther King, Jr.

I had known Martin Luther King's father and mother for many years, always meeting them at the Baptist Conven-

122

tions. His father, the Reverend Martin Luther King, Sr., was the pastor of the Ebenezer Baptist Church in Atlanta, Georgia. His grandfather, the Reverend A. D. Williams, had turned that church into one of the leading houses of worship for Atlanta Negroes.

It was 1955. The great Supreme Court decision of 1954 had declared that segregation in the country's public schools was unconstitutional, and that set the White South to boiling. The Negroes down there were stirring and coming to life, too.

Just before Christmas, a widowed Negro seamstress named Mrs. Rosa Parks had been brought to trial in the Montgomery police court because she refused to move out of her seat in the Negro section of a Cleveland Avenue city bus so that a white man could sit down.

Arresting Rosa Parks turned out to be a spark that was to set fire to a mighty conflagration. There are about fifty thousand colored people in Montgomery and the day when they brought Mrs. Parks to trial about twenty-five thousand Negroes refused to ride on city buses by way of protest. The next day about ninety percent of the Negroes in the city had joined in the bus boycott.

Young Negro ministers led by Martin Luther King, Jr., had joined together to lead the way. They had organized the Montgomery Improvement Association with the Reverend Abernathy as president and they worked through the colored churches to raise money to get car pools organized so that the Negroes could get to their jobs.

That day in Denver, Reverend Abernathy and Reverend King talked to me about the Montgomery Improvement Association. They asked me if I might be able to come down to Montgomery to sing at a rally to raise some money. It was easy to see that Reverend Abernathy was a brave young preacher who wasn't afraid of any man no matter what his

123

color. As for Martin Luther King, Jr., he is not a big man in size but he is a giant in spirit. He always talks quietly and calmly but I could feel his power and his strength.

I told them I would be pleased to come down to Montgomery. I stayed at the Reverend Abernathy's little white frame house. The Abernathys got out of their own beds and gave Mildred Falls and me their beds—they are that kind of people—and Mrs. Abernathy cooked us good, plain food. We ate greens, corn bread and ham hock and prayed together and went off to the church to sing.

They had the rally at the Methodist Church in Montgomery because it is the biggest in the city. The performance was not supposed to start until 8:00 P.M. but the Negroes had been coming in since early afternoon and they had set up loudspeakers in the streets for the overflow crowds.

Police were all over and cars full of white men raced back and forth trying to make trouble, but they couldn't stop the rally. We sang and the ministers spoke and it was a great success and the white people knew it. They began to fight the colored people in the meanest ways they could find.

I hadn't been gone two days when a bomb blew out the living room and the bedroom in the Abernathys' house and they began dynamiting the churches and homes of Negro ministers and some whites who sympathized as well. Colored women with little children to support were fired from their jobs and men were told to get out of town.

But the Negroes, led by Reverend King and Reverend Abernathy, kept on fighting. They had only their churches and their homes to work from. They kept on walking and boycotting the buses all that winter and the next summer, too.

As it turned out, as one newspaperman wrote, "Montgomery is a legend that was written by cooks, janitors and country people."

Even the older Negroes gradually joined in. The older folks told the leaders of the Montgomery Improvement Association, "You call us to a meeting and we will come, even through a den of lions. We are going to stay in this fight until the walls of segregation come tumbling down."

There was a story that went around the South about the Montgomery Negro preacher and the old Negro woman he met walking down the road on the way to work while the buses went past. He asked if she wasn't too tired to walk the long distance every day and she answered, "Before, my soul was tired. Now, only my feet are tired because my soul has found peace."

The bus lines began to become desperate for money because of the boycott. They charged twice as much fare for the white passengers who still rode them and tried running the buses over different routes, but they went deeper into debt. The next year the Supreme Court handed down a verdict that segregation in buses was going against the Constitution.

The Montgomery bus boycott stirred the Negroes down in the Deep South even more in some ways than the Supreme Court decision about the schools. It showed them what they could do and it gave them hope. There was to be no turning back.

Out of the Montgomery Improvement Association came the most important Negro movement since the NAACP—the idea of meeting the white man with nonviolence and passive resistance that Mahatma Gandhi had followed against British rule in India and which Martin Luther King, Jr., preached.

After my visit down to Montgomery I got to know Martin Luther King, Jr., real well. When he came to Chicago to make speeches for rallies and raise money among the Chicago Negroes to continue the fight down South, he and his ad-

125

Senator Hubert Humphrey and I had a lot of fun when we met at the reception given for me in Washington by Under Secretary of State Chester Bowles. *Columbia Records*

visers and friends would often meet together at my new house. We all sat down and ate together and we got to be good friends.

Listening to those colored leaders talk in my home right there in my own living room in Chicago I learned a great deal. I realized I had lived to see a new day dawn for the American Negro and history was being made. I rejoiced that I had a chance to be a small part of it and join in it as a Negro and as a church-going Christian.

The more I saw of Reverend King, the more it seemed to me that the Lord had specially prepared this one man with the education and the warmth of spirit to do His work.

After the Montgomery fight was won, Martin Luther King, Jr., moved down to Atlanta to the Ebeneezer Baptist Church. It became his headquarters when he founded the Southern Christian Leadership Conference, which was dedicated to spreading his preaching that the colored people must gain their civil rights by nonviolence.

The white folks in the South had formed the White Citizens Councils to fight against integration and they worked on the Negroes to make them feel their cause was helpless. They tried to oppress them and defeat their spirit. They kept telling them, "You ain't nothing and you didn't come from nothing!" and the young people were hurt by it.

I remember that during that time I was honored with a reception in Washington, D.C., at the home of Mr. and Mrs. Chester Bowles, and then sang a concert at the Constitution Hall, where Marian Anderson had been barred in 1939 because she was a Negro. This time the hall was pack-jammed with colored folks and they shouted and clapped as I sang "How I Got Over" and "Movin' On Up" and "America."

It was one of the grandest days of my singing career, but afterward there came to my dressing room a little black girl about sixteen years old whose mother was a member of the women's group of the Interdenominational Church Ushers

Association which had sponsored my concert. She waited until all the guests had gone and we were alone and then she said to me with tears in her eyes, "Miss Jackson, how can you sing 'My country, 'tis of thee, sweet land of liberty' as if you believed it when you know the white people in America don't want us here? It's not our country."

She was crying and sobbing. She felt that I was being a hypocrite and that I had let my race down. I began to talk to that poor child. I said, "Yes, honey, it *is* our country, too! We colored folks were brought here long ago and we've been born here and raised our families here. We're Americans as much as anybody else. What we're going through now means better days ahead for you younger people.

"I'm one of the last of the old school of Negroes," I told her. "We had to make it without education. Now you young people have got to get educated. Go back to the school and stay in the church and let men like the Reverend Martin Luther King, Jr., show you the way."

What in the past had been a legal fight by the lawyers and leaders of the NAACP was changing to a great movement of the people. For years the NAACP had been fighting down South to help the Negro get his rights. But now new groups were joining in to march together toward freedom. One group was the young Negroes of the religious seminaries and colleges of the South who had been inspired by the Reverend Martin Luther King, Jr., and by the young Negro schoolchildren who had risked their lives to enter white schools in the South. Besides joining the NAACP and Martin Luther King's Southern Christian Leadership Conference, they formed their own organizations such as the Students' Central Committee, made up of colored students from colleges around Nashville, Tennessee, and the Student Nonviolent Coordinating Committee in Atlanta, Georgia.

There were some northern Negroes among them and some white students, too, but mostly they were southern Negroes

129

—southern-born and southern-raised. These young folks laughed when people like Harry S. Truman, who ought to have known better, declared that they were "Communist-inspired by outside agitators." One student replied, "This is not outside agitation—this is inside agitation."

To these young Negroes segregation is dead. They believe that if they push hard enough they can end segregation in their lifetime and bring up their children really free. It makes me glad that most of these young students know their Bible and they carried it with them on their demonstrations.

Starting in February, 1960, in Greensboro, North Carolina, they began walking quietly into drug stores, dime stores, lunch counters and libraries in the southern towns and cities and sitting down waiting to be served. They called it "sit-ins," and they stuck to the preaching of nonviolence and passive resistance no matter how mean the white people in those places were to them.

They trained each other not to answer back or return blows that the angry whites rained down on them, but to turn the other cheek. Their leaders told them, "You must learn to love those who strike us."

There were still some Negroes who didn't like the idea of nonviolence. They said it was like being like Uncle Tom and letting the white folks whip and beat them. It was still the act of the old-fashioned Negro and they didn't go for it. But they had to learn to understand that, as Martin Luther King, Jr., preached, to be a true follower of Christ you must be nonviolent. No man that represents Christ can be a man of violence. The strong in spirit must bear the infirmities of the way of the weak—that's the teaching of the Bible.

In two years the sit-ins spread throughout the South, and gained for the Negro equal treatment at motion picture theaters, lunch counters, public parks, libraries and beaches in North Carolina, South Carolina, Tennessee and Virginia. More people got involved in the fight for civil rights in one

130

year than at any other time in American history. And I think it was the sit-ins that brought the older people out of their shells. As one man said, "The students go in to stir up a mess and then the older folks have to support them." And with the older people came more support from the colored preachers and the colored churches.

The Montgomery bus boycott had drawn many Negro ministers into the struggle for freedom and civil rights. It gave them the strength to join up. It showed the timid what could be done through the church and it gave them hope. They began to follow the example of preachers like Reverend Abernathy and Reverend King. And more than that— the Negro sit-ins made the country pay attention to what was going on.

11

The Star-Spangled Banner

When the presidential campaign got rolling in 1960, Martin Luther King, Jr., was taking part in the sit-ins that had spread down into Georgia. In the middle of October he was arrested in Atlanta, and sentenced to serve four months at hard labor at the Georgia State Penitentiary.

Negroes all over the country were aroused, and the long distance telephones were buzzing. I was in New York when I got the news and I managed to get through to Mrs. King, who was going to have another child. She was terribly upset and fearful about what might happen to her husband in that state prison and hoping that they might do something up in Washington, D.C. But President Eisenhower did nothing and Vice-President Richard Nixon kept his mouth shut.

Then we got the news that out in Chicago presidential candidate John F. Kennedy had picked up a telephone and called up Martin Luther King's wife himself. He had told her how concerned he was and promised he would do something. That afternoon his brother, Robert Kennedy, telephoned down to Georgia and spoke to the judge who had sentenced King to jail. The next day Martin Luther King, Jr., was set free.

In the Negro world the word of what the Kennedys had done spread like a brushfire. There was much bitterness

132

about President Eisenhower and Richard Nixon's keeping silent and Negroes began jumping on the Kennedy election bandwagon.

Martin Luther King's father is an old-fashioned Baptist who is just naturally wary of the Catholic Church. Like many other Negroes, he had been cold toward Kennedy and intending to vote for Nixon, but now he switched over and said, "This man was willing to wipe the tears from my daughter-in-law's eyes. I've got a suitcase full of votes and I'm going to take them to Mr. Kennedy and dump them in his lap."

On Sunday, Negroes in churches across the nation heard the story of what the Kennedys had done while the Republicans did nothing. From then on the colored votes began going for the Democrats. I've been told that across the country, seven out of ten Negroes are believed to have voted for Kennedy. In Chicago the colored people went for Kennedy by about four to one and in Detroit it was about six to one.

Illinois was carried for the Democrats by only 9,800 votes and about 250,000 Negroes in that state voted for Kennedy. Michigan was carried by only 70,000 votes and again 250,000 of the total votes cast in the state were cast for Kennedy by the colored people. The telephone calls for Reverend Martin Luther King, Jr., by the Kennedys turned out to be one of the most important events of the presidential campaign and the politicians in both parties found out that the Negroes were a force to reckon with.

Voting the Democratic ticket was nothing to me. I've been a Democrat since the days of the New Deal. For twenty years I've been singing and hollering around the Second and Third Wards on the South Side of Chicago for people like Congressman Fred Dawson. That man has opened so many doors to Negroes in Illinois. He has chosen to stay in Chicago and help his people there.

Dawson has not so much the gift of gab as the gift of

Duke Ellington and I work out the rhythm while recording for
"Black, Brown and Beige." *Columbia Records*

getting things done. Once when I was having a hard time making enough money to get by he told me that I was so big and strong that he'd like to recommend me for work as a policewoman. I told him that I was afraid those delinquents would be too much for me. I felt I might curb delinquency better with a song such as "Let Us Walk Together, Children" than with a badge. Many of those that were young and wayward had gotten to know me and I was able to walk down many a dark alley around Chicago without anybody ever laying a hand on me.

The election excitement was just calming down when I got a telephone call from Hollywood. It was Peter Lawford, the motion picture actor, calling. He explained that they were planning a big Inauguration gala celebration in Washington for President Kennedy and it was to be produced by Frank Sinatra. He invited me to come and sing "The Star-Spangled Banner" for them.

I told him I'd love to come. I had never sung "The Star-Spangled Banner" in public before so I began to take time off to practice it in my kitchen in Chicago. The week of the Inauguration Mildred Falls, my piano accompanist, and I got on the train with Congressman Dawson and Mayor Daley and John Johnson, the publisher of *Ebony* magazine, and rode off to Washington, D.C., in great style.

When Mildred and I went around to the District of Columbia Armory, where the gala was to be held, that great big place was just jumping with dozens of entertainers rehearsing songs and dance steps and stagehands hammering and sawing and stringing up flags and banners.

Mildred and I could scarcely believe our eyes. Frank Sinatra and Peter Lawford had gotten American show people to come home for the Inauguration from all over the world. There were Milton Berle and Jimmy Durante and Joey Bishop. There were singers such as Nat King Cole and Harry

136

Belafonte and Ella Fitzgerald and theater people such as Bette Davis and Frederic March.

Up in New York City they had closed down two hit shows so that Sir Laurence Olivier, Anthony Quinn and Ethel Merman could have the night off to be in the gala. Leonard Bernstein was conducting the orchestra. Motion picture people such as Tony Curtis and Janet Leigh had flown in from Hollywood. Ella Fitzgerald had come all the way from Australia. Sidney Poitier had crossed the ocean from Paris and Gene Kelly had come from Switzerland. There was to be an audience of twelve thousand people.

Everybody was rushing around the Armory trying to find Peter Lawford and calling out "Hey, Frank!" to Frank Sinatra, but in the midst of all the confusion he was sitting around as cool as could be. When they heard I was going to be in the gala, a lot of people had warned me, "You'd better look out for that Sinatra—he's supposed to have so much temper," but he kissed me on both cheeks and was as nice as anybody I ever met in the theater or television. I said to myself, "Is this the lion that's supposed to chew me up?" and got over being nervous.

Things were strenuous but everybody worked hard at the rehearsals. We learned all our songs and routines and everything would have been perfect if it hadn't been for the Washington weather that was lying in wait for us.

The gala was to begin at 9:00 P.M. on Inauguration Eve. In the middle of the afternoon it began to snow and by suppertime the flakes were coming down so thick you couldn't see across the street. Washington traffic began to pile up and the autos and buses and streetcars were skidding around and getting stuck all over the city.

Mildred and I barely made it to the Armory. We were worried about being late but when we got there we found out things were at a dead stop. The entertainers were sitting in snowdrifts all over town. Leonard Bernstein finally got there in a police car. He was wearing Harry Belafonte's shirt, which he said was two sizes too big for him, and some of the actors and actresses had to go on in their street clothes because they couldn't get back to their hotels to change.

Long after 9:00 P.M. the audience began to trickle in, glittering with jewels and furs. At 10:00 P.M. President Kennedy arrived to take his place in the center balcony box but when he found that people were still delayed, he chose to wait in a backstage room so the rest of the audience would have time to fight their way through the storm. With him it always seemed to be good manners and consideration for the other person.

Finally, at about 10:30 P.M., Leonard Bernstein led the seventy-piece orchestra in "Stars and Stripes Forever" and then, as President Kennedy entered his box with his whole family, they broke into "Anchors Aweigh."

Everybody was standing up cheering and applauding. Bugles blew. Spotlights hit the side entrances and in marched all the famous actors, actresses, singers and dancers as the orchestra played "Walking Down to Washington," which had been specially written for the occasion. It was as thrilling as a big nominating convention and had me tingling all over.

Then the theater lights dimmed down and I stood up to sing "The Star-Spangled Banner." I always sing with my eyes shut, so I couldn't see how the audience liked it but people said I sounded fine.

The big show with skits and dances and singing lasted until almost two o'clock in the morning. Then we all went to a big supper that Frank Sinatra had arranged for the entire cast. It was a lovely party that looked as beautiful to me as a biblical revelation. I met the family of Vice-President Lyndon Johnson, who were very, very sweet to me, and the President's father and mother.

About 3:00 A.M. I was sitting at my table when I saw a

138

tall young man in a blue suit coming my way. It was the new President of the United States and he had come over by himself to thank me for opening up the gala and tell me he had known my singing for a long time and always enjoyed it.

He shook my hand and I thought to myself, "This skinny young man has got a grip that makes you feel his strength!" and then he looked into my eyes as if he was looking right into my soul, and I suddenly knew how he was able to draw people to him in a magnetic way. He made me feel as if I was a part of his life and time.

The same feeling came over me the next morning when we all sat down in the bleachers and wooden seats in front of the Capitol to see our new President take the oath of office and to hear him deliver the Inaugural Address.

It was bitter cold even with the sun shining, but as he spoke nobody moved. It was as if people felt they were part of a great moment and when the President finished his speech, they applauded it like they were trying to make their hands talk.

I thought to myself, "I feel that I'm a part of this man's hopes. He lifts my spirit and makes me feel a part of the land I live in."

Suddenly I felt that we Negroes who were fortunate enough to travel abroad to other countries could answer foreign newspaper reporters' questions about segregation and integration because now we had a President who really believed in equal rights and had it in his heart to do something about it.

All that day of the Inauguration while the bands played and the parades marched by there seemed to be a new spirit in Washington—a spirit of jubilee. Everybody felt excited and proud about being there and it was a great moment for Americans. I haven't changed my mind about President Kennedy since then and I never will.

12
Tell the world about this

After the Inauguration Mildred and I took to the road again on a concert tour that ran from New York to Texas. Most of the time we drove from city to city in my car. I've often been criticized for owning a Cadillac, but if the people who did the criticizing knew anything about one-night-stand concert tours, they'd understand why I have that car.

The one-night-stand concert artist has to be stronger than a Mississippi mule. You finish singing about eleven o'clock at night. You're too keyed up by the evening to go to bed but you're in a strange town and by that time even chatting with the nicest visitors is a strain. No matter how much you love the public and the public loves you, they sap your strength. You just want to be alone with one or two close friends.

Most of the time you can't make a good train or plane connection that will carry you anywhere near where they have booked you to sing the next night. The best thing to do is get in a good car and go. It has to be a big, fast-driving, easy-riding car so that you can get your rest. Sometimes we leave town right after a concert and sometimes we sleep and get out after an early breakfast, but we spend most of the time between concerts on the road.

I used to drive a lot myself but now I usually engage a cousin or friend to come along with us and do the driving

140

and handle our bags. This time out we did two months of one-night stands until I felt like that big car was fitted to me like a tight corset. Meanwhile, mail was flying back and forth between our hotels and Chicago about plans for another concert tour in Europe. I said I would go if I could get to see the Holy Land. That was my big reason for going, so they booked me into a tour of six European countries with a trip to the Holy Land tacked on the end.

Mildred Falls was to go with me as my accompanist and Al Duckette, a young Negro reporter, signed up to handle the press and television people. I gave a last concert in San Antonio, Texas. We drove straight through to Chicago to put the car in the garage and then caught the train to Washington, D.C.

In Washington there was a bon voyage reception for me at the home of Under-Secretary of State Chester Bowles. I had come to know both Mr. Bowles and his wife through my concerts and they were most interested in my European tour.

There were some newspaper reporters at the reception who wanted to know if the State Department was sending me on the tour. I told them I didn't need to go as a representative of the State Department; I was going as an Ambassador of God, but I was honored by the party and I felt humble to see how I was graced by the love of so many Americans and so many people from other countries, too.

There was another wonderful reception given for me by my colored church friends in Washington and then we hit out for New York and went aboard the *United States*, which was sailing for Europe. A lot of my oldest friends came down to see me off. Ernestine Washington, the gospel singer who is known as "The Songbird of the East," was there and so were a lot of gospel singers such as Marian Williams of the famous Ward Singers. They had flowers and champagne for us and big baskets of fruit, and I summoned up my last

Once I'd begun flying in airplanes, it wasn't so bad. Here we're arriving in Amsterdam, Holland. *Combi Press Service*

strength to say goodbye as the ship's whistle began to hoot and everybody went down the gangplank.

We sailed down the river past the Statue of Liberty and then suddenly I was taken down with a wave of nervous exhaustion. I crawled into bed feeling weak and frightened. I felt so low I was afraid I would never be able to sing. The one-night stands had sapped my energy and taken my strength. I felt as if somebody had been dragging me across railroad ties.

My mind kept turning back to the first European concert tour I had made eight years ago and how it ended with me being flown home in an airplane to a Chicago hospital. I kept whispering to myself, "Here I go again and I'm going to flop! I haven't got the strength left to make it."

For two days I lay in my stateroom on that big ship without moving. People kept slipping invitations under my door and I just lay there and looked at them. My stewardess was a lovely German woman named Florence. She brought me hot tea and broth and fussed over me to get up and try the ocean air, but I didn't think I could make it.

Then the ship's doctor came in. He took my blood pressure and said it was low.

"If it's low, I'm lower," I told him. "I don't know how I'm ever going to get up on a stage and sing for people."

He laughed and said, "Don't worry, that's one nice thing about a boat trip across the Atlantic Ocean. We've got plenty of time to build you up."

He put me on a diet of steaks, spinach and grapes and told me to drink a glass of wine every time I ate. After another day or so I began to feel myself coming back.

It was the first time in my life I had ever been out on the ocean on a big liner and I never knew I loved the water so. I sat up on a high window seat in my cabin looking out at the sea and listening to the sounds the waves made as they swept past the ship. It was peaceful and soothing and I sat there by myself for hours.

After a while the rest revived me and I went out and mingled at a party for Jackie Gleason. He was on his way to Europe to make a motion picture and it looked as if he had rented half the boat, he had so many folks traveling with him. He and I got to talking and I found he had a lot of soul. He told me all about the movie he was going to make in Paris. It was called *Gigot* and he was going to play the part of a deaf mute who was trying to show the powers of God although he could not speak. I could feel by the way he spoke about it that he was going to make a strong picture.

Within an hour I was back again in my cabin sitting on the window seat, watching the beautiful sea. I never knew water had such a drawing power on me. It was wonderful to see the different shapes the waves took as they passed by and to hear the different sounds and rhythms they made. I sat there and looked out at the sky and the sea and I felt almost transported.

Florence, my stewardess, kept bringing me in things to eat and drink and she would say, "Goodness, are you looking at that water again?" and I would say, "Yes, I do enjoy it so much. I'm fixing to stay right here until we get to Europe."

But finally Mildred and Al wouldn't let me stay inside any longer and coaxed me to try a stroll around the decks. They both had been having a wonderful time visiting around the ship and they wanted me to join in. We met one of the original Mills Brothers—Mr. George MacArthur—who now has a regular job on the *United States,* and then we went to the big dining room and had dinner with George Wein, whom I had met when I sang at the Newport Jazz Festival— before it got to be a beer festival and I quit singing up there.

On Sunday I came out again for the church service and sang "Were You There When They Crucified My Lord?"

145

Right in the middle of it the boat began to do some heavy rolling and I could see Mildred was getting seasick and I felt it, too, but we rode it out and finished the hymn.

Now the ship-to-shore telephone calls began coming in for me from the English newspapers. The boat began to bustle as we got in sight of land and the stewardesses and the ship's nurse and the cabin boys came to say goodbye and tell me all the places I must not miss seeing.

At the dock there was David Haber, the young man from the William Morris Agency who had made all the arrangements for the tour. He had two cars waiting for us. One was a station wagon and the other was a long, black limousine with a chauffeur for us to ride in all the way to London.

It was raining and at first I was worried about the people driving at us on the wrong side of the road but then I began to enjoy the scenery. All along the road there were beautiful sights to behold—lovely flower gardens and green grass and beautiful homes with terraces and landscaped hedges. It was wonderful to see so many of the English people riding bicycles and just walking easy along the road, just the way people did down South when I was a little girl.

After we got closer to London, however, the sights disappeared. The road went bad and that car about whipped me to death. It was a great big famous English limousine but it shook like it had no shock absorbers and I couldn't have felt any worse if I had been riding in a wheelbarrow.

The first thing we had to do in London was record a television program. We didn't have much time to rehearse but the English musicians who worked with me were wonderful. Their choir sounded almost as good as an American Negro church choir. Their musical arrangers knew their music so well that they just listened to Mildred and me run through a number and then put it all down on sheets of music and got it all right.

There was a young singer named Leon Bibb on the program with me and he has such a fine voice that I felt he was headed for an important career. I tried to make myself flexible and friendly with everyone and we had a good time together.

The next evening was the moment that I had been building myself up toward for a long time. It was the night of the concert at Albert Hall. The last time I had sung at Albert Hall I had felt so sick I had scarcely been able to stand up and I felt that time that the people who came to the concert had not been moved and that big hall had beat me. Ever since I knew about this new European tour I'd had Albert Hall on my mind and it had worried me. It was what had made me feel low and fearful when I sailed from New York and I was still eating liver and spinach like a prizefighter getting ready for his big fight.

The morning of the concert I woke up feeling weak and exhausted again but I prayed a bit and felt a little better. I was tense and wanted to get out to the hall and come to grips with it. I kept begging everyone to hurry. We got there in the daylight so that I had a chance to walk around outside and see what a great, statuesque piece of architecture it is.

The hall was named in memory of Prince Albert, who was Queen Victoria's husband. He died while he was still a young man, and the young Queen went into retirement and did not appear in public for years. When she came back into public life, she built the Royal Albert Hall in his memory and it has become one of the greatest concert halls in the world. The first time I saw it I thought it looked like it was built before Jesus came—it has that old, reverent look about it.

We went inside to look over the stage and I remembered how the last time I had been there in 1952, the ramp that led up to it had looked like a mountain to me because I was so weak.

Mr. Christopher Howes, the manager of the hall, came

to greet me and make everything into a warm, pleasant atmosphere, which helped me to build my hopes for the evening. Mildred and I went back to a little room to rehearse a bit and when Mildred began playing "The Love of God," I felt the tears starting to come.

I was crying with happiness. I felt all in a glow and in a hurry to get out there on that stage. I knew I was going to be able to do it. I told Mildred to let her heart take courage and not let anything disturb her because the Lord had given us another chance.

David Haber came rushing back to tell us they were selling standing-room-only seats and that Princess Alexandra was in the audience, but it didn't frighten me. I felt holy that night and grateful to God. And so the time came. And Mildred walked out on the stage first and took the piano and got a wonderful hand of applause. Then I came out and stood there looking at what the Lord had done for me—looking out at the great hall filled with a great audience. It didn't seem to threaten or challenge me. I had a feeling of victory—that the Lord had brought me to stand there and He was there with me that night. I felt that I was singing to God and the Lord's spirit was upon me.

We started out with "My Home Over There," a gospel song that I have always liked to sing because it reminds me of the Apostle Paul when he said, "I've fought a good fight and kept my faith." When I sing it, I always think of the day

> When my work is done,
> Set the setting sun
> And I'm going to my home over there.
> I shall walk the golden stairs
> And be free from every care,
> When I reach my home over there.

I believe that one day I shall do that.

The last time I had sung at Albert Hall the audience had

been cold as ice but this time there was a difference in them because there was a difference in me. Here in Europe I had found out the strength of the Lord and what the Twenty-seventh Psalm really meant.

We did the concert in two parts—the first part with me singing an hour steady plus encores and then, after a rest, coming back to sing for another hour.

There may have been more than religious people out there in the audience—jazz fans and rock-and-roll people. I couldn't say who was there and how many were saints or sinners. But when I sang the songs of God—slow, reverent songs and songs with a driving beat—the reception they gave me was like a religious revival audience. They carried on with such cheering and whistling and stomping that somebody called the police. When we came out through the stage door, the waiting crowd surged forward like an army. I got knocked down and had to crawl the rest of the way into the car on my hands and knees.

At the hotel, David and Al and Mildred got me some hot milk and food and put me to bed to sleep. But after they were gone I switched on the light and opened my Bible and read for a while and then I got out of bed and knelt down and thanked God for his blessing. My body was so exhausted that I didn't make it a long prayer but it was a sincere one. I knew now that the rest of my European tour was going to be a success.

The next day we left England on a Channel steamer with the seagulls behind us sweeping over the white cliffs of Dover. We whizzed through Belgium on the Trans-Europe Express until we got to Frankfurt, Germany, for a concert at the Kongresshalle, which is a modern building, all glittering with glass and chrome but with nothing to back it up.

The piano sounded tinny no matter what Mildred did with it. The stage steps felt rickety under my weight. The dressing room was cold and unfurnished. The microphones

European audiences have always been wonderful to me, even when they don't understand the words of my songs. This is in Stockholm, Sweden. *Ture Skölander*

were no good and the lights were terrible. The manager there was just the opposite of the Englishman at the Albert Hall. He was full of rudeness and bad temper and wouldn't even give us a broom to sweep up the stage.

David Haber began to splutter at the manager—he said later he never knew how well he could speak German until he found he could lose his temper in it—and I chimed in, hollering that if this was what Germany was going to be like, they could just cancel me out.

After we let him know what we thought of him and his hall we felt better about it and gave the concert anyway. The German audience turned out to be wonderful. I did ten or twelve encores and went back to the dressing room and changed into a skirt and blouse and came out and sang some more. Again, they wouldn't let me go home until the police were called. Everybody shoved and pushed and shouted and David Haber accidentally got punched in the jaw and all messed up.

After he got me safely into the car, I told him, "You forgot to tell me you need a strong body when you go on a concert tour in Europe, not just a strong throat! These people are going to mob us to death." But I really appreciated it because the white American audiences sometimes act like they got blisters on their hands or are afraid to be seen applauding. Over there in Europe they clapped and pounded and cried "Bravo!" until they made me dizzy.

Later on at a party some of the Germans who could speak English remarked that they had been quite surprised by my singing and found the style of some of it quite different from my records that had been issued a couple of years before. I told them they were right about those records being different. The record company had stuck me with a musical director who had me doing arrangements that were jazzed up and doped up with a heavy beat. Sometimes they

152

even cut choral groups and violins into the tapes after I had recorded them and when the album came out it sounded like I was singing with a whole bunch of people. When the Germans heard me without a band or fancy arrangements—just standing out there flat-footed singing from the nub with Mildred at the piano—they liked it much more than they did those juiced-up records.

Making a good, honest record of a person's voice depends a lot on the engineers in the studio sound booths. It is harder to hold a big voice to get the beauty out of it than it is to magnify a small voice. If you get an engineer who squeezes your voice, he can leave out all the depths. Some of those studio engineers have made me sound like a pig squealing under a gate.

We went on to Hamburg to stay at the Atlantic Hotel on Alster Lake, which was beautiful with sailboats, and there I had another dream of my life come true. When I was a child working in the white folks' homes around New Orleans with my aunt Duke, I often helped out in the kitchens when they had the big dinner parties. I can still recall how the lady of the house used to come out to the kitchen and worry us all to death about her crystal ware. "Child, be careful of those glasses!" she would say. "They're imported from Europe. They're as precious to me as jewelry." I used to get so nervous that I was afraid to pick up a glass for fear it might slip through my fingers and the house would fall on me.

Now here I was in Hamburg, which is a crystal city. The Lord had fixed it so I could walk right into those big, famous stores and buy crystal for my own home back in Chicago. We went to Latorrf's, which is one of the grandest places in the city, and I bought crystal goblets and sets of beautiful glasses for wines and punches and champagne so that even though I wouldn't be doing much drinking myself I could have the pleasure of serving my party and dinner guests in high style. Then we bought porcelain sets for serving coffee, and mugs and cake dishes.

On the way back to the hotel we spotted some pastry that looked too good to pass by. We carried it back to my room and took off our shoes and ate cinnamon rolls and jelly cakes and looked out at the boats on the beautiful lake, making it one of the loveliest and most restful days I can remember.

The Hamburg Musikhalle, in which I sang that night, was perfect. They had a wonderful piano for Mildred and again the audience overwhelmed us. They were standing on the steps in the balconies, sitting on the floor and leaning up against the pillars with their eyes closed, transported by the gospel songs. I finally closed the evening with "The Lord's Prayer" and went back to my dressing room to change clothes, but the cheering and stomping never stopped.

Mildred went out to play for them and hold them while I finished changing. I just had time to zip into a brown street dress and slip my feet into some Indian moccasins before the whole audience was carrying on for more singing.

I walked out on the stage and said, "All right, if you don't mind me singing in my Indian shoes that I bought in Window Rock, Arizona, here we go!" and Mildred and I gave them the best we had left in us.

13
Keep a-movin'

We had done three big concerts in a row and I was tiring.
David Haber began to get after me about flying around
Europe instead of taking the train. "If the Lord is with you,"
he said, "let's fly. That way you won't get exhausted."

I reminded him my contract said I didn't have to fly but
I said I would pray on it and let him know. Then on the
way to Berlin we hit the Russian Zone, and it must be the
worst train ride in Europe. The tracks were bumpy. The
food was stale sandwiches that stuck in your throat, and
Russian soldiers in steel helmets kept climbing on and off the
cars at every stop. I gave in and told David, "I've done made
up my mind. I'm going to take to the air. The Lord heard my
prayer and let me know what to do. From now on we'll fly
around this continent."

In Berlin the concert was at the Sportspalast. During the
ovation the concert manager mentioned something that made
me shiver. The great crowd was chanting and cheering and
he said the last time he had heard them chant that way was
in 1938 when Hitler had delivered a speech on the same
spot. I shuddered to think that Hitler had stood there and
cried for war. Now, years later, I hoped I was able to reach
the young people with my songs and help them feel peace

and the love of God. They certainly seemed to understand and accept my gospel singing.

The next day was a nervous day for me because we were going up in the air. It was a Pan American plane, and when we got aboard the pilots and stewardess came by to say hello and joke with me about flying. We swooped up into the sky and I was doing my best to let go the sides of my seat and relax when the pilot suddenly came on back and sat down to talk some more with me. The only words I could get out were, "If you're back here, who's looking after things up in the front?"

He laughed and said, "Oh, we've got another pilot and a co-pilot, too. Come on up and see for yourself."

I thanked him but told him I wasn't moving until he got us back down to the ground.

When we landed in Denmark at the Copenhagen Airport, the reporters were out to meet us. One man wanted to know if I had had a hard time in America because of my color. My answer was that I had had a hard time all my life but not just because I was born black. I felt he was trying to make something bad about my country for his headlines.

There was not much point, it seemed to me, in going around Europe talking about the race problem in the United States. We have to solve our problems ourselves back home. If the white man in the South is against the Negro, there is still no need for me to go around everywhere saying we're against him. As a colored preacher, the Reverend B. E. Cox, told a group outside a segregated Howard Johnson restaurant in Durham, North Carolina, "We want to say to the good white people here that we are not mad at anyone. We're mad at segregation."

Another reporter told me how much he admired my singing. "I don't believe in God myself," he said, "but when you sing it gives me goose pimples."

"That's not goose pimples," I told him. "That's your soul

156

speaking and you don't even know it's there! You've got to believe in it; otherwise you can't account for the feeling the singing arouses in people. Gospel songs and spirituals are more than just Negro music. There are no slaves in Europe, but people love the music. Why is that, unless it's because it stirs a spiritual need deep within them?"

When we came into the airport outside Paris, we were expecting more reporters and photographers, but the place was almost deserted. We found we had hit into something unexpected. The whole country was under martial law because of the Algerian revolution and everyone was afraid paratroopers were going to drop down out of the sky during the night and march on the city. People who had bought tickets for my concert at the Olympia Theater were calling up to find out if it was canceled.

I was ready to sing, paratroopers or not, and while the concert hall people were making up their minds what to do, Mildred and I went to do some sightseeing. We rode down the Champs-Elysées, which everyone said was the most beautiful street in Paris, and then drove out to visit a place that to me was even more exciting—the white stone church called the Church of the Sacred Heart. Its pure white walls and sculptures and stained glass windows seem to sing with the beauty of joyous worship.

Then we went on to the Cathedral of Notre-Dame and I saw something I had never seen before. There was a statue of Jesus rising out of the grave, telling Mary Magdalene to go and spread the gospel. I felt my knees go weak and just stood there holding onto the gate that protected the statue, staring at it, feeling that I could never bring myself to leave. The memory of coming upon it will be mine forever.

On the way back to the hotel we passed the Eiffel Tower and the Louvre Museum and drove along the banks of the Seine River. Mildred and I agreed that we didn't know anything about the Algerian revolution but we owed the paratroopers a vote of thanks. Because of the commotion over their coming, we had a chance to see much more of Paris than we would have otherwise. I've been to Europe twice and they have rushed me from concert hall to concert hall so fast that I still haven't had a chance to see much of it.

As it turned out, the worst thing I had to face in Paris was not the paratroopers but the Olympia Theater. The sound equipment was bad. The piano was a poor one. The dressing room was small and the theater was old and run-down. The whole thing made me feel very low. I felt that I had worked for years to escape from singing in such places and here I was back again.

The concert manager who had booked my European tour had been dodging me all over Europe; but that night of all nights he made the bad mistake of visiting me at the Olympia. We had quite a talk in that dingy, crowded little dressing room. I was blood mad and dished him out good. He might think he owned a lot of American singers, I told him, but he didn't own Mahalia.

I managed to forget about him when I walked out on the stage and the French people gave me the kind of greeting that only they know how to give. It makes you feel as if you could stay in Paris for the rest of your life. The theater was hot and I had to work hard to overcome the microphones but it was a rewarding evening. Afterward, Hugo Panassie, the French music critic, and Milton Mezzrow came back to the hotel and we visited for hours talking about our singing friends and musicians and the many changes since our first meeting.

When I had come to Europe on my first tour in 1952, nobody there (and not many in the white world in America) knew anything about genuine gospel songs. Since then gospel music has gone commercial in a big way. There are dozens of Negro gospel groups touring around the country. Some of the singers are young folks who were trained by great

158

singers like Clara Ward and by me when I was going to different cities to hold revival meetings in the tents and churches. They have some of the most exciting new voices in America. They want to be heard and they are tempted into singing in nightclubs and restaurants. But I think when this happens Satan is stepping in.

There is a principle to singing gospel music and to me it's a mockery to religion to sing religious songs to people who are drinking and dancing. I find myself asking, "Are you still singing to build up God's kingdom?" They tell me there has even been a group going around singing a song called "The Gospel Twist," but I can't bring myself to discuss that kind of a mess!

My one big disappointment in Paris was that I wanted to get some French lace curtains and a tapestry for my home, but there wasn't time for another shopping trip. I had to rush on to sing again in Germany—in Munich and Essen.

In Essen there was another one of those cold-looking modern halls like the one in Frankfurt, but the audience had all the warmth of the human spirit in them. They kept calling me back over and over again for encores until there was Mildred in her street dress and me in my brown skirt and Indian moccasins, with nothing else on the stage. They had even taken away the microphones to get the crowd to leave, but nobody budged. They were calling out to me in both English and German and someone explained, "They want you to sing 'The Lord's Prayer' before you go."

This touched me very deeply and I sang it for them without any microphones, just leaning up against the piano as Mildred played. The silence of the people as I sang was something I shall always remember. It seemed to convert that cold, hard-looking modern hall into the most sacred kind of place.

In Zurich there was a dinner with the U.S. Consul General, Mr. Robert Peters. He had recently been stationed in the

I was reluctant to fly on my European tour, but I realized that the Lord would take care of me. *David Haber*

Mildred Falls and Al Duckett and I visited Saint Peter's at the Vatican. *David Haber*

Middle East and got me excited with his stories about Jerusalem and the Holy Land. My concert tour was finally coming to an end and soon I would be on my way to Jerusalem.

Our route carried us by way of Italy and Rome for a visit to the Vatican. We got to Rome in the middle of the day and found there was no place to eat. The Italians had closed down most of the restaurants so that they could take an afternoon rest. I was told they do this for three hours after lunch every day and the idea appealed to me. In France we had found that they close a lot of their stores on Monday, just the way the colored people in New Orleans used to have "Blue Monday" when nobody went to work, and it seemed to me a nice way to relax and enjoy life a bit rather than the wild way everyone rushes around in the big cities back in the States.

After a night's rest we went around for our visit to St. Peter's Basilica. It's the largest church in the world, and whether you're a Catholic or not, you can't help but be struck silent when you see it, it's so magnificent.

The main altar is solid gold with beautiful statues and carvings. The one I shall always remember was the *Pietà*, carved by Michelangelo, which shows the Virgin Mary holding the crucified Jesus across her lap.

When the great church was filled, a procession started with the Swiss Guards of the Pope in red-and-yellow-striped uniforms and then the Pope's own attendants in black uniforms with shining silver helmets—and finally Pope John himself. He was wearing a pure white robe and was borne above the crowd in a gilded chair carried by men in brocaded costumes. He gave all of us present his blessing, and although I am a Baptist I found myself moved by a deep religious feeling.

The next afternoon we went back to the Vatican for another visit. An Archbishop O'Connor led a group of us through a huge room that was furnished with red chairs and red curtains and had a marble floor that shone like a mirror. Then the Pope walked in, again dressed in white robes and looking wonderfully peaceful and holy. He spoke to us quietly and beautifully in French and a monsignor translated it for us, explaining that the Pope was asking us all to think of his St. Peter's as a mother with outstretched arms calling the young to her bosom and how important it was not to ignore the bad that is present in the world but to labor to make the evil into Godliness.

Again, it seemed to me that I was in the presence of a truly good man—a man of God—and his words spoken to us there in that old city of early Christian faith so filled with churches and statues and places like the Colosseum, where the first Christians were fed to the lions, had great meaning for me.

A train carried us to Naples and we went aboard a lovely little Italian ship called the *Esperia* which sails from Italy across the Mediterranean Sea to the Middle East.

14
Walk in Jerusalem

In the Egyptian port of Alexandria the noise and heat and mixed-up smells were so great that I thought I would never eat again. The shops with the pieces of meat hanging outside and the flies buzzing did not appeal to me—I'm too used to having a fit about keeping a clean kitchen—and I also could have done without seeing the five-thousand-year-old mummy they showed me, with its toes still sticking out of the shroud.

We landed in Beirut, Lebanon, in confusion and traffic. I had thought the taxi drivers in Rome would give me a nervous breakdown, but you have to see the Middle East to see people really go crazy with automobiles. While the American consulate people went all out to help with the arrangements for us to drive through Lebanon and Syria to Jerusalem, the U. S. Marine Guard invited us over to their quarters for a luncheon of American-style stew and made a fuss over us that made us feel right at home. Then we were ready to set out up into the mountains for the ride to Damascus.

Baalbek—a temple that the ancient Romans erected in the desert over two thousand years ago—loomed up in front of us and we stopped to wander amidst the silent ruins of the great columns that still reached up toward the sky. I could feel the past of ancient times descending around us like a great cloak and I had the sense of being at last in the land of the Old Testament where the tribes of Israel had fought and wandered—every moment was exciting. In Damascus I found myself gazing at the church of St. Annanais, where Paul himself had preached, and at St. Paul's Church I saw the window where he had let himself down in a basket to escape.

We got up early in the morning to take to the famous road that leads through the desert from Damascus to Jerusalem. It was here Paul had been thrown from his horse and blinded by God, who had cried out to him, "Why dost thou persecute my people?"

It was a wild, narrow, dusty road, no wider than a strip of hall carpet, and we drove down it through the fierce heat in an old touring car with our bags piled high up on top. The driver they had picked for us was a great big Arab man who wore a red fez and right away he and I began to have a time together. Syria has the worst driving people in the whole world and they must have picked "Fez" as the prize of the nation. We went shooting out of town with him pumping brake fluid and going at breakneck speed down the mountain roads.

I can't ride in the back of a car because it makes me dizzy so I had the seat right beside him; it was like being in the front seat of a roller coaster. I kept a good grip on my Persian lamb coat with one hand. The other I kept free to poke him until he stopped accelerating. We went racing down through the desert with me poking and hollering and him telling me he had never been treated that way before by any woman and he would like to come to the United States and marry me. I told him he had missed his chance. I would never marry a man who drove a car the way he did.

Before I knew it we had reached the River Jordan. I made "Fez" stop the car and I got out and walked slowly down to that old river and knelt to let its waters flow through my hands. It was muddy brown just the way the Mississippi River is at New Orleans but much cooler even in the blistering heat of the desert.

A little bit farther on we passed the Dead Sea and then reached the hills of Jericho. On the slopes strewn with stones were barefooted Bedouin children with shepherds' crooks, herding sheep and goats, veiled women with earthenware jugs balanced on their heads and tribesmen in turbans. Their sheep and camels settled down in the yellow dust of an old dried-up river bed and I found myself exclaiming, "Why, it's all still the same! That little boy tending the sheep could be David! Those women could be Naomi and Ruth on the way to the well. That old man could be Abraham or Methuselah. I'm seeing it all just as Jesus did, with my own eyes!"

Here in the Holy Land I had reached one of the most important moments of my life. When I was younger and singing about the glories of Jerusalem, I had always thought it was only a place in heaven. Later on, when I found it was a real city, I remembered an old Negro spiritual:

> I'm going to walk in Jerusalem—
> Talk in Jerusalem—
> Shout in Jerusalem—
> Pray in Jerusalem—
> High up in Jerusalem—
> When I die!

Now here I was about to walk the same streets where Jesus walked, and to pray at Calvary, and see all the things I had always sung about. This was my second homecoming!

The next day on a morning that was soft and sunny we drove through the deep-cut hills of Galilee along a road that was crowded with ox-carts, donkeys and people traveling on foot until we reached the little town of Bethlehem. Guides escorted us into a stone courtyard and then into a big arched hall. Here was one of the world's oldest Christian churches standing on the site of the inn in which Mary and Joseph had sought lodging for the night.

We went slowly down a steep flight of stairs and they left me alone to pray in a candle-lit chamber in which there was a rock that is said to mark the spot where stood the manger in which Christ was born.

It came to me then that the first gospel singers were the angels who sang here on this spot of peace on earth and good will toward men—of joy to the world because our Saviour had come. That's all gospel music is—just an expression of joy and hope. That's the way the songs have always seemed to me all the years that I've been singing them.

Later that day Mildred and I entered the walled garden of Gethsemane. It was fragrant with flowers, and silent monks from the old Church of St. Anne were tending its gardens and bordered paths. There was the grove of olive trees, all twisted and gnarled, some of them believed to be two thousand years old, among which Jesus had prayed with Peter and suffered the agony of the spirit as He prophesied that before morning He would be betrayed.

Then, on foot, we slowly followed the guide through the hot, narrow, stone-cobbled streets of Old Jerusalem, filled with the strange wailing sounds of Arab music and crowds of people, all shopping, shouting and crying out their wares just as they must have been doing for thousands of years since the times when men were fighting there with spears and swords. I found myself unable to speak as we walked over the same path that our Lord had been driven along by Pontius Pilate's Roman soldiers bearing His cross.

Finally, in the coolness of the chapel in the Church of the Holy Sepulchre, trimmed with gold and rubies that shone in the flickering candlelight, the guide showed us a tiny marble chamber.

"Is this it?" I asked him.

"They believe this is the place," he said quietly.

167

In the Church of the Holy Sepulcher I realized that my dreams had come true, and I felt truly blessed. *Ali Za'Arour*

All my life I had wanted to go to the Holy Land. This snapshot was taken in the Garden of Gethsemane. *Ali Za'Arour*

I knelt down and stayed there alone trying to find the words for a prayer of thanks. My dreams had come true. With my own eyes I had seen the place where Christ was born, and with my own hands I had touched the Rock of Calvary. Everything was drained out of me. In the old Hebrew of the Bible my name, Mahalia, means "Blessed by the Lord," and truly, it seemed to me, I had been blessed.

Later, while I was resting at the hotel, a reporter came to visit. "What message are you bringing to the Jews of Israel from America?" he asked me. "What songs will you sing here?"

"I'm going to sing the same gospel songs I've always sung," I answered. "I'm not fixing to change my singing just because I'm singing in Israel. I'm going to bring the Jews Christ."

Well, we really got going on that one!

That reporter was a poor German Jew whose family had been abused and sent to the gas chambers by the Nazis and he didn't have much faith left in anybody. He told me he didn't have much use for Christians. Everything evil that had happened to him and his family had been done by Germans who called themselves Christians. "How can you worship a Christian God," he asked me, "when the white Christians have abused you Negroes so much, too?"

I told him that in his bitterness he was forgetting how many people God had disposed of for the Jews of the Old Testament.

"Think," I said to him, "of all the Philistines and Pharaoh's Egyptian armies that God had destroyed for the sake of the Jews!

"To my way of thinking, those old Jews had been disobedient toward God, and Moses and Elijah had to go and pray to God to forgive the old Jews' sins. So don't put it all on the Christians who don't practice the Ten Command-

170

ments," I said. "Some of the tribes of Israel had broken them, too.

"I'm reminded to tell you," I said, "that when Paul was writing for the Corinthians to the Church of Rome he wrote that God was not only the God of the Jews but the God of the Gentiles as well. And through his son, Jesus Christ, God had fulfilled the promise of the Old Testament. There is nothing between God and mankind since the coming of Jesus. The Jews are still hunting for a Messiah," I told him, "when he's already been here and ascended back to Heaven."

Well, that man turned out to be a good sport about me letting off so much steam. He said he was the son of a line of seven rabbis so he wasn't about to change his religion, but nobody had talked to him quite like that before and he would think it over.

As things turned out we had a fine concert in Israel in a hall in Tel Aviv. The people packed into a big auditorium and I sang for them "Didn't It Rain?," "I Found the Answer," "He's Got the Whole World in His Hands" and "When the Saints Go Marchin' In."

For two hours the people, lots of whom could not understand the words, followed along with me and some joined in hand-clapping and praying. We had a good time—Jews, Arabs and Christians—all of us together.

Back in my room I fell on the bed feeling worn out by the concert tour and the emotional strain of my visit to the Holy Land.

I was ready to take the next plane out and fly back to France to catch my ship, the *United States*, which had carried me over to Europe three months before. Once again I rested, sitting in my cabin window seat or out in a deck chair, just watching the ocean go rolling by. I let my mind run back over all the things I had seen in Jerusalem and thought it would be wonderful to go back again someday, not to sing concerts but perhaps to act as a missionary for my church, and perhaps pay a visit to Egypt to see the land of the Pharaohs.

When we steamed into New York it was just at dawn and the sun came up to blaze on the city's tall buildings and make them look like towers of gold.

When we docked, the bands were playing and there was a great uproar. Standing at the rail, looking down at the pier, I could see the shining faces of many of my old friends who had come all the way from Chicago and Washington and Philadelphia to greet me. I could see them before they saw me and suddenly I got a very strong feeling. It came to me that this was the way Heaven might look to me—that there, too, might be the music and many people waiting for me—my mother, who had died when I was such a little girl; my father, who loved me so; my aunts, who raised me; and the wonderful ministers, who have meant so much to my life—all of them and many more wonderful people who had passed on might be waiting for me just as in the song, "In the Sweet Bye and Bye, We Shall Meet at the Beautiful Shore."

I was back home again and I felt that when my time came, Heaven would feel like this, too.

15

If we never needed the Lord before

The spirit of peace that had come to me from my visit to the Holy Land was shattered by the news that swirled around me like a storm in New York and Chicago after my return to America. It was all about a group of young people, both white and colored, who belonged to the Committee for Racial Equality and who called themselves Freedom Riders. They had decided to challenge the way the South was still treating colored people in the intrastate bus terminals. The Supreme Court had ruled in 1956 that these places must no longer be segregated but we all knew that the southerners were still forcing Negroes to use separate waiting rooms and keeping up the White and Colored signs in the terminals' restaurants.

In Washington, D.C., the Freedom Riders got aboard a Trailways bus headed for New Orleans and they stayed on it while it rolled deeper and deeper into the South. The news of their coming spread ahead of them, and when they got to Alabama, crowds of white men were waiting for them. They were met with such violence that some were hospitalized with terrible injuries. But they had kept going.

When I went visiting down to that part of the South a little later on, I was to hear how a riot at the Montgomery bus terminal had touched off a great protest demonstration among the colored people of the city, and how our gospel music had given the people courage and spirit when they were in danger. Once again, mass meetings were held at the Negro churches as they had been when Montgomery was fighting the battle of the bus boycott. The Reverend Martin Luther King, Jr., and the Reverend Ralph D. Abernathy came up from Atlanta, Georgia, and a special evening service was held in honor of the young Freedom Riders at the First Baptist Church on Ripley Street.

At suppertime the colored people of the city began to move toward the church. The white mobs were out in full force and as Negroes got near the church they were struck by rocks and stones. Some of their cars were set afire and bombs were set off, but the Negroes kept right on coming. They filled up the church and began singing hymns and gospel songs.

After the police force of Montgomery had stood by and let the white gangs attack the Freedom Riders at the bus station the federal government had ordered in a force of one hundred U.S. marshals to keep law and order. The marshals lined up in front of the church while the white crowd built up in a park across the street. Yelling at the colored people to come out, they began to close in on the marshals.

Inside the church the people could hear the mob coming closer. They began to sing "Love Lifted Me Up!" and the Reverend S. S. Seeay, chairman of the meeting, cried out, "Come, now! Everybody sing as if he believes it!" and the people sang louder and louder.

Outside the marshals were shooting off tear gas bombs to hold back the whites. Highway police rushed toward the church with sirens screaming. The wind blew the tear gas fumes inside the church and some of the older people began to get frightened. Women were moaning in the heat and

174

smoke and choking and getting ready to break down into panic.

The Reverend Ralph D. Abernathy rose up to cry, "We don't have to sweat and gasp in here! Those U.S. marshals are supposed to protect us. Open the windows! Let the fresh air in! Let those outside hear us sing a little louder!"

The people began to sing with more spirit, "Leaning on His Everlasting Arms." While they sang, the Reverend Martin Luther King, Jr., went down to the basement and telephoned to Attorney General Robert Kennedy, who was standing by the telephones in Washington. "They are moving in on the church," he said. "Are you going to stop them?"

"We will stop them," Kennedy answered.

On another telephone he was talking with the Governor of Alabama. A few minutes later the National Guard was ordered to the church. It took almost the rest of the night but by dawn the soldiers had escorted the church people safely to their homes.

The next day the Freedom Riders rode a bus protected by police and soldiers to Mississippi. Again they were arrested and put in jail, but by now the whole world was aroused by the treatment they had received. Like the sit-ins, the Freedom Riders had won a great victory. Once again, the young people had shown the way.

Many more Negroes now were resolved to force open the doors in the Deep South that had been closed to them since slavery times. They listened when Martin Luther King, Jr., told them, "It is ultimately more honorable to suffer indignity than accept segregation in humiliation."

With Martin Luther King, Jr., preaching to him, the new Negro down South began raising up his head and walking just as Jesus had told him to do.

I believe that God has raised up leaders like Martin Luther King, Jr. He can cope with the white man on any ground.

In 1954 I had my own radio show on WBBM in Chicago. Here I am with the Falls-Jones Ensemble—Mildred Falls playing piano and Ralph Jones on the organ. *CBS*

99,000 people came to one concert at Soldiers' Field in Chicago, and what a time we had! *Chicago Tribune Photo*

And he can put up with the people of his own race who cause him trouble, too.

Some of the talky Negroes around Martin Luther King, Jr., have made statements that have been a trial to him. His enemies, both white and colored, have tried to make it seem sometimes that his groups are divided and disunited. Martin Luther King, Jr., has answered only that "the issues are too serious for us to become involved in ego battles and trivial conflicts." If he is tired of his struggle, you would never know it when you talk with him. Martin Luther King, Jr., doesn't show a weary spirit. Some people say he's changed. I don't see any change in him since that day I met him in Denver eleven years ago except that he is more determined and inspired by God than ever.

The leaders of the future are young men like the Reverend Martin Luther King, Jr., who is staying down South and showing the young colored people how to get things done. He's leading the way—just as it says in the Bible: "First seek ye the Kingdom of Heaven and its righteousness and all things will be added to you."

People tell me Martin Luther King, Jr., ought to be in Washington, D.C. I say that's the bunk! Martin Luther King, Jr., is not for politics and the outside show. He knows the Negro in the South still needs teaching and training and he is staying down there to show them the way. He is serving his people.

I had a wonderful opportunity to see one of the reasons for the greatness that is within Martin Luther King when he invited me to join him and his family for Thanksgiving at his own home in Atlanta, Georgia.

I had been making a concert tour through the South. With me was Mildred Falls and my old friend from the gospel tent days, Professor William Frye. After we finished a concert in North Carolina we drove on down to Atlanta and found our way to the street in the colored section where

Martin Luther King lives in an old-fashioned two-story brick house next door to the church he now shares with his father.

From the moment I entered that house I had a wonderful feeling of family warmth that came from seeing Martin and his lovely wife, Coretta, and their three children. Dexter, the youngest, is named after the first church Martin had on Dexter Avenue in Montgomery, Alabama. Little Martin, Jr., and his sister, Yolanda, have that new "look you in the eye" spirit. They are happy children and they don't look down at their shoes the way colored children who have had their spirit hurt often do.

That night Martin took us all out to dinner. Later we went back to the house and before we went to bed we helped Coretta King get things started in the kitchen for the Thanksgiving dinner she was to serve the next day.

When I awoke it was a beautiful soft southern autumn morning. I lay quietly in bed enjoying listening to the King children playing and laughing downstairs and feeling the happy spirit that seemed to flow through the whole house.

During the morning, as the turkey was roasting in the oven, Martin's mother came to join us and then the wife and children of Reverend Abernathy, who has fought side by side with Martin Luther King ever since the Montgomery bus boycott. Abernathy himself couldn't be there because he was up in Chicago speaking at a rally to gain more help for the Negro cause in the South.

When it came time for dinner we all gathered around a big table set with a beautiful white tablecloth. The children took their places and Martin first said a Thanksgiving prayer for peace and then got down to carving the big turkey that Coretta had fixed with all the trimmings. Up and down that beautiful table everybody was passing greens, cornbread, sweet potatoes and a platter of baked ham. Later on we had pie with ice cream and pots of hot coffee.

All during the dinner we talked and joked about little

179

family things and laughed with the children and the dinner had that old-time countryside feeling of an old-fashioned Thanksgiving day.

For anybody who rang the doorbell that Thanksgiving Day Martin Luther King and his wife had a warm gracious southern way of welcoming them in. You might think the threats to her husband and her family would break Coretta King's spirit, but she still carries on.

Truly I felt: Here was a family in which people were thankful for the small things as well as the great.

That night, after we had left Atlanta and headed up into the Great Smoky Mountains toward Nashville, where I was to sing at a revival meeting, I looked back on the pleasant day. I hoped that through the work of men like Martin Luther King, all Negro families might be as happy and full of Thanksgiving some day as the King house had seemed.

It wasn't until later that I realized that during the afternoon when Martin was stepping into his study with some of his callers, plans were being made for another big protest movement in Georgia. And turning on the radio only two weeks later, I heard that he had once again been arrested and sent to jail. Among the many who had come and gone quietly that pleasant afternoon were the men who were planning the Albany Movement.

The Negroes' new fight for rights had come to a new focus down in the heart of the "Black Belt" in Albany, Georgia, where the colored people have never been granted their rights, including the right to vote. Two weeks before Christmas, 737 colored people led by Dr. W. G. Anderson, a Negro doctor from Albany, and the Reverend King, marched together in downtown Albany. They held a meeting and prayed for the white people to please see the light and let them have their rights.

In that great Christmas congregation there were young people, old women in their seventies, working men, doctors, lawyers and housekeepers. They were all arrested and put in jail.

Martin Luther King, Jr., and Ralph Abernathy were convicted of leading the demonstration and went to jail. Later, Reverend King and nine other Negroes were jailed again when they prayed on the steps of the City Hall, but the Albany Movement only grew stronger.

The Negroes began letting the white people know their feelings by not going into the city's downtown stores, and the boycott emptied the streets of shoppers.

Once again it was in the churches that the colored people rallied for their cause. The white people oppressed them and threatened them, but the Negroes would swing into hymns like "We Are Climbing Jacob's Ladder" and "Pass Me Not, O Gentle Saviour" and the song that got famous during the student sit-ins—"We Shall Overcome."

It has meant so much to me that a great part of the brave fight for freedom down South now is coming from inside the church and from the hymns and gospel songs the people are singing.

The "Freedom Songs" began back during the Montgomery boycott when the Negroes began singing in the churches to keep up their courage. When the students began to go to jail during the sit-ins they began to make up new words to the spirituals and hymns and old gospel melodies that the Negroes had been singing in their churches for generations. Some got printed, some got put on records and some just got passed around.

Using songs as a way of expressing protest and gaining strength and hope runs way back deep in the American Negro's past. When the colored slaves on the plantations sang, "Steal away to Jesus, I ain't got long to stay here," they weren't talking just about Heaven; they were expressing their secret hope that they, too, would have their chance to escape up North to freedom.

181

When you come to hear religious music, you're not supposed to feel bigger than anybody else, and white people and Negroes applaud just as hard. *Columbia Records*

The soul of the Negro just naturally has so much rhythm and music in it that "testifying" to music in church and "getting happy" with singing has always been a way in which the Negro has sought to renew his strength.

Now all through the South the Negroes are singing. They sang while they were put in jail by the hundreds and sometimes the power of their music was so great that the white guards began singing right along with them.

They sing in churches and in mass meetings while deputies and sheriffs go around taking names and white gangs burn up their cars.

The big song of the movement that is now sung in the South by thousands of Negroes almost every night is "We Shall Overcome," which says—

> We shall overcome, we shall overcome,
> We shall overcome some day.
> Deep in my heart I do believe
> We shall overcome some day.

The "Freedom Songs" have caught on because music speaks a language to individual souls that cannot always be expressed by the spoken word. There's something about music that is so penetrating that your soul gets the message. No matter what trouble comes to a person, music can help him face it. Some who didn't believe in God have found him through music.

Many colored people in the South have been kept down so hard that they have had little schooling. They can't handle a lot of reading, but as one preacher said, "The singing has drawn them together. Through the songs they have expressed years of suppressed hopes, suffering and even joy and love."

One young Negro leader said, "Without music there could have been no Albany Movement."

184

And Martin Luther King, Jr., said, "The Freedom Songs are giving people new courage, a radiant hope in the future in our most trying hours."

The white folks got so confused by the way the Negroes kept gaining strength that gangs of men began prowling the countryside around Albany at night burning Negro churches. And it is to the everlasting shame of the white Baptist preachers in the South that they have not spoken out loud against these cowardly attacks on a sanctified place.

In fact, when a group of ministers and rabbis from the northern states came down to Albany to let the colored people know they had plenty of support, the white preachers of Albany ran out of town and hid somewhere. And when the ministers from the North were arrested and thrown into the Albany jails for holding a prayer meeting, the white churches of Albany kept silent. It still beats me how a man can go around preaching about the love of God, whom he has never seen, and scorn his brothers, whom he meets every day on the face of the earth!

16
We shall overcome!

Meanwhile, like a mule that has been put back between the shafts, I had been singing my way across America on the one-night-stand concert tour road. I had sung in New York, Kansas City, Los Angeles and Seattle and this time the pace had broken me down.

Lew Mindling, my manager, cut the tour short and took me back to Chicago. He was so worried about me that he insisted I let him put me in a big white folks' hospital over on the Chicago "Gold Coast," where the North Shore millionaires live.

"Are they treating you all right?" he asked, when he called on the telephone the next day.

"They're treating me too much!" I told him. "They've stuck me so full of needles I'm like a pincushion, and they've given me so many pills that my voice is so high that I sound like Lily Pons!"

The doctors found that I didn't have cancer and I didn't have TB, but they discovered I did have diabetes and they said my heart was strained and tired from the many years on the concert road. They were all as nice as they could be to me but I couldn't rest easy. One night around midnight, I slipped out of bed and got into my clothes.

"Where in the world are you going?" the night nurses asked.

"Home," I said. "The Lord has told me to get up and get on back to my own bed. I'll take my treatments there."

All I could do for the rest of the summer was rest. My concert dates were canceled and I couldn't even get out of the house to go to church. I would lie on a couch and talk long distance to people like the Reverend Martin Luther King, Jr., and he would say, "When are you coming back down South where there is so much going on?" and I would say, "I can't come yet. In the shape I'm in here, if you get me arrested in one of your demonstrations and put in one of those Georgia jails, I'll never make it to the outside world again. But give me a little time and I'm going to sing for you—somewhere—someday."

I never could have guessed then how my promise would come true—how on a lovely summer day in August, 1963, I would find myself in Washington, D.C., standing beside Martin Luther King on the steps of the Lincoln Memorial watching tens of thousands of Americans, black and white, go marching into the pages of history books, as we all took part in the March on Washington for Jobs and Freedom.

It was that grand old leader of the Negro civil rights fight, Philip Randolph, who had first proposed the march more than a year before. Back in 1941, Philip Randolph had helped President Franklin D. Roosevelt push the first Fair Employment Practice Committee bill through the Congress by talking about bringing thousands of Negroes to Washington to protest about job rights. This time he wanted us to come to Washington to speak out in one mighty voice for equal rights for ourselves and our children.

Old Philip Randolph worked for nearly a year on the plans for the march and, looking back now, it's hard to believe that people dragged their feet as much as they did. In the beginning, colored people as well as white talked against the

187

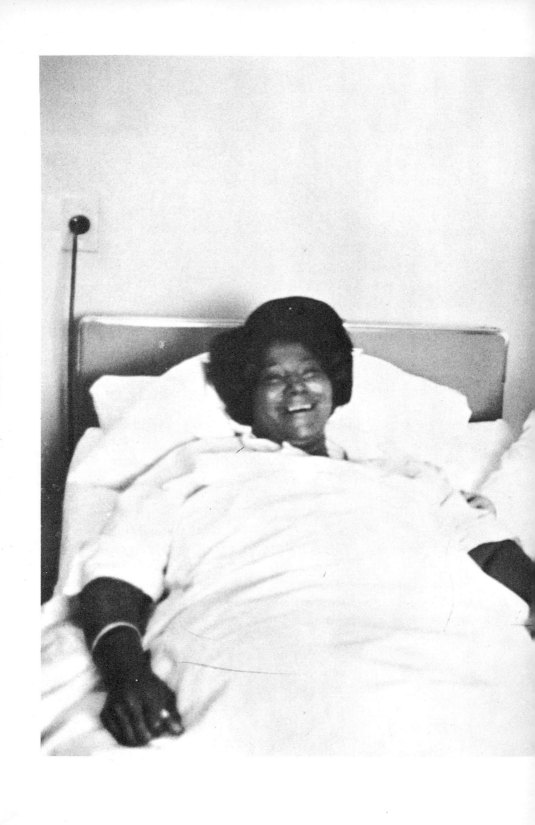

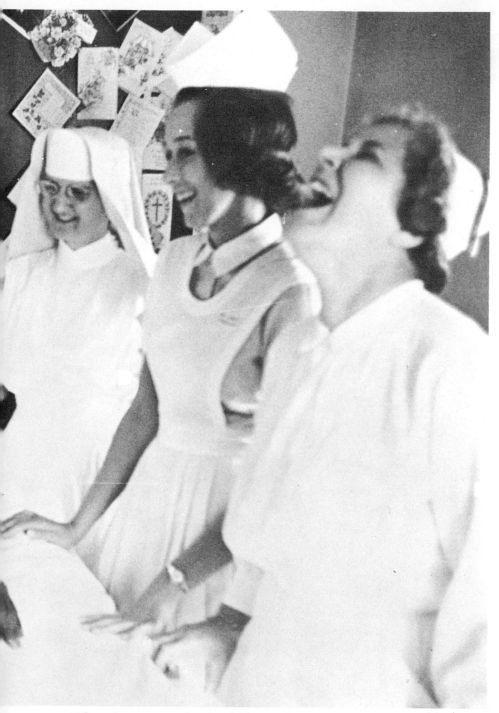

When I was so sick, the folks at the Little Company of Mary Hospital were as nice to me as could be. *Johnson Publications*

march. Everybody told Philip Randolph it would never work —you just couldn't expect people from all over the country to leave their jobs and pick up and go to Washington. And they said that anyway it would be a waste of time for all of us to come because the Congress wouldn't pay any attention to us.

As for the white people, you could tell just by reading the newspapers that most were against the march. It looked to a lot of them like just another case of a bunch of Negroes looking to draw attention and stir up trouble. In a way, of course, they were right, because as one man said later on, "The American Negro has decided he has to *annoy* the white man to wake him up."

No matter how hard everybody tried to get Philip Randolph to call off the march, that strong-willed old man wasn't about to change his mind. Instead he just pushed that much harder. He got bright young colored men like Bayard Rustin to help him with the organizing, and he traveled day and night across the country getting church groups and union groups and young Negro student groups to promise they would join in. The more put out the white people got about the march, the more white newspapers talked against it, the more determined the Negroes seemed to become. All at once, march talk was all you heard in Negro beauty parlors, barber shops, in the churches and at the lodge meetings.

When the white folks in Washington realized we were really coming, a lot of them got frightened. Some were so sure that there was going to be violence and rioting that they locked up their houses and ran clear out of town to hide out in their country places over in Maryland and Virginia.

And it was no wonder that the white man was afraid. During springtime demonstrations for civil rights, Negroes— men, women and even children—had been sent to jail by the thousands. They had been beaten up, bombed out and blackjacked by white people, and the guilt of the white people for what they had done and allowed to be done was strong in the South as well as in the North.

Driving into Washington the night before the march, it looked to me like we were entering a city that was about to be captured by an enemy army. Houses were dark and the streets were deserted. There were so many patrols of police and soldiers around you'd have thought the Russians were coming.

When we got to the hotel the first thing I did was find one of the men who were in charge of the march program.

"What about tomorrow?" I asked. "Are we going to have a good crowd? Are people really going to come?"

That man was really excited. "Are they coming!" he cried. "Mahalia, you're going to see a sight tomorrow like you never saw before. They're going to be rolling into Washington all night long by bus, by train and by the carload.

"There are five hundred busloads coming down from New York and eighteen special trains coming from the South and from the Midwest. They're coming in by plane from New Orleans and California.

"There's a bunch of young CORE people who have walked all the way from New York City. There's a man who's come all the way from Chicago on roller skates and an old man— eighty years old—who just rode in from Ohio on a bicycle. There are going to be young folks, old folks and not only colored people but white people too—thousands of them!"

When I woke on Wednesday morning I found that God had blessed us with a beautiful day. It was sunny and bright, not a hot, sticky Washington day but a crisp, breezy kind of summer day that just made you feel good all over.

When we drove downtown we found that an army had come to Washington during the night, but it was an army of gentle people. There they were—tens of thousands of them!

191

—spreading out on the grassy slopes and under the big elms and oaks in the big park between the Washington Monument and the White House.

Families were getting out folding chairs, opening picnic baskets and spreading blankets on the grass. Mothers were feeding tiny babies. Fathers were taking their children up to the top of the Washington Monument and walking them up to look at the beautiful fountains playing on the White House lawn. Boys and girls were racing around playing tag. Old men were sitting quietly playing checkers.

It looked like some kind of a big picnic or outdoor church rally. Almost everybody was dressed up. You never saw so many coats and ties and best blue suits and black dresses and Sunday bonnets. You could tell just by looking at them that these were church people—good people who were thinking about their families and their country. Ministers were everywhere and everywhere you could hear "Good morning, Reverend . . . Good morning . . ."

The police and young soldiers who had been called out stood around looking puzzled. They had been told to be ready for riots and here they were surrounded by people who were saying "Excuse me" and "Good morning" to them and carrying nothing but water jugs and Bibles.

There was nobody to arrest—no fighting—no shouting, pushing and shoving. It was as if the human race had taken a day off from being mean to each other. Here were black and white people that had come in peace—united by a spirit of good will and sweetness and dignity.

Everywhere there was a spirit of happy, joyous celebration as if the day of Jubilee had come. It had me dazzled. It filled me with pride and made me feel so uplifted that I was brimming over ready to shed tears and laugh at the same time.

I got out my own camera and started taking pictures.

There was a lot of buzzing going on about the many

celebrities, both white and colored, that had come to stand up and be counted. Josephine Baker and Sidney Poitier had come from Paris. Jackie Robinson, Harry Belafonte and Lena Horne were with groups from New York. Whole planeloads of actors had come from California. Before the day was over I had snapped pictures of Marlon Brando, Sammy Davis, Jr., Burt Lancaster, Paul Newman, Charlton Heston and Dick Gregory.

Besides the big names from show business there were all the Negroes who had fought so hard for civil rights in the Deep South. There was Mrs. Medgar Evers, whose husband had been killed in cold blood by a shot in the back fired by a white man in Mississippi, and Daisy Bates, who led the first colored children into a white school in Little Rock, Arkansas.

There were the Sunday school classmates of the little children who had been killed by a white man's bomb in a colored church in Birmingham and brave preachers like Reverend Fred Shuttleworth, who has shown the courage of a lion in helping his people stand up to the white racists in Alabama. There were all the young students, many of them fresh from southern jails, who had marched against snarling police dogs and tear gas, guns and clubs in Alabama and Mississippi.

For many of the Negroes that had come from the Deep South, it was the first time in their lives that a white person had gone out of his way to be really nice and courteous and friendly to them. It was the first time a lot of them had ever laid eyes on Washington, D.C. For the old folks it was probably the last glimpse they would have of the beautiful city and I thanked God they saw it on such a lovely day in all its shining beauty.

All morning, as the charter buses and special trains kept pouring into town, the crowds grew larger and larger. When they added it up later it was found that two hundred thousand Americans, white and colored—the largest protest

193

Ambassador Ralph Bunche showed me around the United Nations on one of my trips to New York. It's wonderful to know how hard those men are working for peace for the whole world.

crowd that had ever come to Washington—had joined in the great march.

Soon the singing began and all through the throngs of people you could hear the stirring melodies of old spirituals and church hymns and the new Freedom Songs. People gathered in groups to sing "We Shall Overcome," and "We Shall Not Be Moved," and "Before I'll Be a Slave I'll Be Buried in My Grave and Go Home to My Lord and Be Free," and "Blowin' in the Wind."

Just before noon when it came time for the last stage of the march, there was a great surge toward the Lincoln Memorial. People streamed into the two great avenues bordering the beautiful reflecting pool that runs between the Washington Monument and the Memorial.

It was a parade that you see only once in a lifetime. Thousands were walking twenty abreast singing hymns and songs, waving American flags and banners and signs about the Civil Rights Bill, flowing like two great rivers toward the Memorial. There were old folks in wheelchairs and men and women on crutches. I saw a white man help a colored woman who was marching alone with four children. He picked up one child and they all walked along together.

To me it was like marching with a mighty host that had come for deliverance. I kept thinking of the words of the Bible—"And nations shall rise up . . ."

And it seemed to me that here was a nation of people marching together. It was like the vision of Moses that the children of Israel would march over into Canaan.

After we got to the Lincoln Memorial I climbed the marble steps to where the great statue of Abraham Lincoln sits looking out over Washington and took my seat in a wooden chair to listen to the speakers introduced by Philip Randolph and await my turn to sing for the marchers.

The summer sun was beating down on us but I never gave it a thought as I sat looking out at the great sea of people and banners, spread out as far as I could see. I couldn't look hard enough or long enough. The beautiful day and the great multitude gathered there had such a special meaning for me that I felt as if I were hypnotized. I was living and breathing history.

I myself was the granddaughter of Negro slaves who had labored on a Louisiana plantation. All around me were the great Negro leaders of my own generation—men like Philip Randolph and Roy C. Wilkins—and the new young leaders like Martin Luther King and Whitney Young and John Lewis who with the help of the young Negroes were bringing about another revolution in American history. Sitting and standing side by side with us were white people—Catholic, Jewish and Protestant clergymen and union men like Walter Reuther.

Near me sat Dr. Ralph Bunche, who had raised the American Negro to a new eminence in the United Nations, and Thurgood Marshall, now a federal judge, who, as an NAACP lawyer, had waged the case against segregated schools until he won the famous Supreme Court decision in 1954.

Here on these same marble steps Marion Anderson had sung in 1939 after being rebuked and barred from Constitution Hall by the white members of the Daughters of the American Revolution.

I thought back on how in the fifty years since I was a child on the Mississippi levee I had seen my people and my country move forward in so many ways until now we were at the threshold of salvation.

It seemed to me that despite the hatred and fears Negroes still had to face, the American people were beginning to fall into step with us and the hopes for days to come seemed as bright as the sunshine that sparkled over the Potomac River and shone on the tall Washington Monument.

With a truly exalted feeling I rose to sing. I'd thought long and hard about what was the right song for me to sing that day. It had been Martin Luther King who gave me the answer. When he heard me talking about it, he had said, "Mahalia, why don't you sing 'I Been 'Buked and I Been Scorned' for us?"

There's probably only a few white people who ever heard of that song, but it's an old spiritual that is known to colored people up and down the land. It was exactly the right choice for the day because its words reflected the depth of feeling of all the colored people who had come to Washington and it would reach out to all the millions who might be watching and listening to us on radio and on TV.

At first I sang the words softly . . .

> I been 'buked and I been scorned.
> I'm gonna tell my Lord
>> When I get home.
> Just how *long* you've been treating me wrong.

As I sang the words I heard a great murmur come rolling back to me from the multitude below and I sensed I had reached out and touched a chord.

All day long I had been going back and forth between tears and laughter. Now I wanted to let the joy that was inside me about this day come pouring out. I was moved to shout for joy. I lifted up the beat of the rhythm to a gospel beat.

I found myself clapping my hands and swaying and the great crowd joined in with me with a great wave of singing and clapping.

I had my new hat pinned tight on my head so I could let myself go. I could sway and bounce as much as I wanted and Mildred Falls at the piano went right along with me.

People were joining in to sing with me. All through the great crowd I could see their hands clapping and people who had been dipping their tired feet in the long reflection pool began to splash and rock to the rhythm.

Flags were waving and people shouting. It looked as if we had the whole city rocking. I hadn't planned to start a revival meeting but for the moment the joy overflowed throughout the great rally.

They said later my singing seemed to bounce off the golden dome of the Capitol far down the Mall and I've always hoped it reached inside to where some of those Congressmen were sitting!

I had scarcely sat down and caught my breath when Martin Luther King was on his feet delivering a speech that was to make him famous.

In his speeches and sermons Martin Luther King never lets himself go in the shouting and stamping style of an old-fashioned Baptist minister. It's just not in his nature to reach the people that way.

Although he has become the most beloved and respected and powerful Negro leader in America, he is still a quiet-spoken man who can preach a whole sermon without getting his collar wet.

But on this wonderful afternoon the pride and joy he felt about the great march and the spectacle of that multitude of people with all the hopes they cherished for their children carried him away, too.

"I have a dream," he cried out to us, "that one day on the red hills of Georgia the sons of former slaves and sons of former slaveowners will be able to sit down together at the table of brotherhood.

"I have a dream that my four little children will one day live in a nation where they will not be judged by the color of their skin but by the content of their character.

"I have a dream one day that little black boys and little black girls will be able to join hands with little white boys and white girls and walk together as sisters and brothers.

"This will be the day when all of God's children will be

able to sing with new meaning, 'My country 'tis of thee, sweet land of liberty, of thee I sing,' and 'From every mountainside, let freedom ring.'

"And if America is to be a great nation this must become true. So let freedom ring from the prodigious hilltops of New Hampshire. Let freedom ring from the mighty mountains of New York. Let freedom ring from the heightening Alleghenies of Pennsylvania! Let freedom ring from the snow-capped Rockies of Colorado! Let freedom ring from the curvaceous peaks of California! But not only that; let freedom ring from Stone Mountain of Georgia! Let freedom ring from every hill and mole hill of Mississippi. From every mountainside, let freedom ring.

"When we let freedom ring, when we let it ring from every village and every hamlet, from every state and every city, we will be able to speed up that day when all of God's children, black men and white men, Jews and Gentiles, Protestants and Catholics, will be able to join hands and sing in the words of that old Negro spiritual,

> Free at last! Free at last! Thank God
> Almighty, we are free at last!"

It was the greatest speech of the day and when it was over, everybody was all used up.

"Go home," Philip Randolph told us. "Go home and continue the fight in every nook and cranny of the land."

As quietly as they had come the great crowds began to steal away. The last songs died away. By evening the last of the special trains and chartered buses were pulling out of town. Some of the people that had come from the Deep South had twenty hours of bus riding ahead of them, but as one old woman said, "We've had the biggest day of our lives. When I get home I'll be ready. I don't care whether it's picketing or marching or a sit-in, I'll be ready to do it."

Over at the White House, President Kennedy congratu-

200

lated Philip Randolph and all the other march leaders on the way the day had gone. We had shown the white man that the American Negro has as much dignity and thinks as deeply as he does. We had let Washington feel the weight of our determination. We left in triumph but we left as we had come—with peace and good will to all.

I may not live to see the complete freedom that Negroes seek come to America but I got the vision of it that great day.

President Kennedy already had done more than any other American president to make the American Negro feel that Washington, the capital of the United States, belonged to him as much as to any white person.

It had often seemed to me when I traveled around Europe and talked with people from so many different countries that Americans back home didn't really understand how much the rest of the world loved and respected our President. His greatness didn't really dawn on them until that terrible day in Dallas, Texas.

I was in California that November morning, just leaving my hotel to drive to a television show rehearsal, when Mildred Falls came running to say, "They just said on the radio that President Kennedy has been shot!"

None of us could believe it. We got into the car like we were numb and started for the TV studio, saying over and over again to each other, "It can't be. It must be a mistake."

Then just as we got to the TV studio we heard everybody saying, "He's dead."

"Oh, no, Jesus!" I cried out. We turned the car around and I made it back to the hotel and knelt down on the floor beside my bed. I could hear the President's voice as if he were in the room with me. All the memories of the many times I had seen him and listened to him talk, since I'd first noticed him as a young senator at the Chicago Convention in 1952, came flooding over me. Everything he had said and done to

At the March on Washington, I began to sing softly, "I been 'buked . . ." *Ebony Magazine*

Then I was moved to shout for joy, and I lifted the rhythm to a gospel beat. The great crowd began singing and clapping, and joy overflowed. *N.Y. Daily News Photo*

help all Americans, black and white, find their way came to my mind.

I gazed down at my clasped hands and thought, "To think that these old working hands of mine that washed and ironed and took care of so many children were held by such a great leader! To think that now such a great young man has died to help set colored people free!

Later on Martin Luther King said, "This is what the poison of hate will do!"

I, too, will always believe that President Kennedy gave his life for the colored people. He stood in the way of a bullet the same way he stood against hate.

The Oswald boy may have fired the shot but he did no more than what he had seen other older people do—shooting Negroes in cold blood, killing little Negro children in a colored church in Birmingham, Alabama, with a bomb!

The Oswald boy may have killed the President but it was the sins of the Americans who spend their lives hating that helped him aim the gun. How could Oswald believe that it was wrong for American to go against American when he saw the South block Kennedy and speak with such hate against him?

Hate in America has been like an epidemic. How many more will go down before it as if they were struck with a terrible disease? How many more will hurt and kill and do the things that are whispered about down in Mississippi when even white preachers and judges hate and hide and protect each other so that no one can get at the truth? Let them all try to throw it off on the Oswald boy! The sins and transgressions of the South against colored people—the sponsorship of hate and evil—had much more to do with the killing of our blessed President.

When President Kennedy died, he grew even greater in death.

Great leaders like young John Kennedy are born. I believe now he couldn't help himself. It was his fate that he had to die and his family had to suffer for the need of this country to find its way back to its senses.

God can't find too many strong men that are willing to give up their lives for the common people. It was not just political ambitions that moved President Kennedy to press for colored people's rights. It was something in his heart. It was something he was always talking to Americans about—the way a young preacher talks: "Forget about yourself! Live together as one! Ask what you each can do for one another!"

As the songs say, the truth of his words will go marching on.

17
Just as I am

One of the people who was a comfort to me in the days of deep sorrow I went through after the death of President Kennedy was a tall, soft-spoken colored man named Sigmund Galloway.

At the time he was living in California, where I was spending so much time making recordings and singing at concerts. It wasn't long before my old friend and manager Lew Mindling, who always has his eye on me, was asking, "Who's your stage door date, Mahalia?"

"Date!" I'd exclaim. "What you talking about? Can't a nice man drive me home and take me out to dinner without you spoofing me about dates?"

My marriage to Ike Hockenhull had ended when I was only thirty years old and from then on I never got serious about another romance.

I used to joke with my Negro audiences at concerts and church meetings, "Out of all the good-looking men I see here tonight I ought to be able to find myself a husband!" But I never intended it as anything but a little joke. I made the church and my singing the heart and soul of my whole life.

I had known Sigmund Galloway's family through the Baptist church for a good many years. They lived over in

Gary, Indiana, where I often went to sing, and they were good church people. When I first met them, Sigmund was married and had a little girl named Sigma. Later his wife died and Sigma went to live with his mother.

In the beginning I knew only that Sigmund was in the building business. He had learned the trade from his uncle, who had made a specialty out of building better homes for colored people around Gary.

Later on I discovered that music was an important part of Sigmund's life, too. He liked both popular and church music. He sometimes played in an orchestra and he did some arranging, too.

That winter of 1964–65, when I was spending so much time in California, Sigmund was with an orchestra in Los Angeles, and when he found out that I was there, too, he began to come to see me and started going to my concerts. He was always ready to encourage me after I had had a long tiring recording session or concert. For the fun of it, we worked out some new arrangements of my gospel songs together.

At first I was taken with him because he was such a soft-spoken man with a kind way about him. One day I suddenly realized he was tall and handsome, too. I began to look forward to our dinner dates more and more, and felt proud to ask him to take me to parties and dinners I was invited to attend in Hollywood.

By the time I left to make another concert tour in Europe I was calling him "Minters," which was his family nickname, and I could tell he enjoyed being with me as much as I liked him.

The month I spent in Europe kept me too busy to do much more thinking. I was singing gospel concerts in Holland, which is a very religious country, and the people came out to see me in such crowds that I was swept off my feet by the excitement. Everybody seemed to know about my songs

207

Mr. and Mrs. Sigmund Galloway. *Ebony Magazine*

I hate to see the songs that have been the strength of the colored people jived up by the commercial world. *Ebony Magazine*

and my records and it pleased me so much to see so many young people crowding into the concert halls in Brussels and Amsterdam to listen so eagerly to the old spirituals and gospel hymns.

Then suddenly the excitement of the tour was all over and once again I was sailing for home on the big liner, the *United States*.

As we crossed the Atlantic Ocean I found myself thinking a whole lot about my future life and about Minters Galloway.

I knew all about the joys of a wonderful career which had made me famous; but I knew, too, about how empty and lonely life could be when I came home from the big tours to my house in Chicago. For years I had been traveling so much that, although I had friends all over the United States and Europe, in Chicago I was alone a lot of the time.

I loved my house and I'd enjoyed furnishing it in the nicest ways I could, but when the door shut after a dinner party I was alone. In recent years I sometimes had felt a loneliness that was strange to me. Sometimes when I was home in Chicago, weeks passed without my once going up to the front of my house to use the parlor.

· As I sat gazing out at the ocean I found myself wondering what it would be like to be married and have a home to come to instead of just a house. The more I thought about it, the more I thought about the good times I had been having with Minters.

I thought to myself, "I'm not going to ask him but if he starts coming around to see me in Chicago, he'd better watch out!"

Then I thought to myself, "*You'd* better watch out! You were married once and now here you go again!"

It was about two months later that I called Lew Mindling on the phone in California. "I've got something I want you to do for me in Chicago," I told him. "I want you to come back here and give the bride away."

"What bride?" Lew asked.

"Me," I said. "Minters asked me and I accepted. I'm going to get married!"

Lew got so excited he almost disappeared off the phone.

"Didn't I tell you!" he cried. "I knew those 'dates' of yours were getting serious."

"You knew it before I did," I answered laughing.

Lew got on a plane and the next afternoon a quiet little group of us got together in the living room of my home. I was still feeling tired from the tour and I didn't feel strong enough to have a lot of people and photographers around.

I put on my best blue dress and wore a corsage of white orchids. With Polly Fletcher, my secretary and friend for many years, and Lew Mindling as our only guests, Sigmund Galloway and I were married in my living room by the Reverend Leon Jenkins, pastor of the Greater Salem Baptist Church.

After it was all over, Polly began to cry a little, but I stopped her.

"From now on," I said, "this house is going to be a happy *home!*"

To celebrate, we went downtown to the Top of the Rock restaurant way up on the roof of the Prudential Building, where you can sit and look out on all Chicago.

While the waiters were pouring champagne I was holding Sigmund's hand and gazing out on the lights of the city which had been such an important part of my life. I heard a voice saying, "Let's drink a toast to Mrs. Galloway."

"Who is that?" I asked, without thinking.

I looked around and Lew and Sigmund were laughing.

"That's you," Lew said. "And you'd better not forget it so soon!"

Mahalia Jackson Galloway!

Once again I was moving on up into a new life with my hopes for happiness always a little higher. Along the new way I would rejoice with the Lord and sing my gospel music.

There are still some people who will try to tell you that gospel singing is a fad and that it will fade away. Don't you believe it!

Gospel music is nothing but singing of good tidings—spreading the good news. It will last as long as any music because it is sung straight from the human heart. Join with me sometime—whether you're white or colored—and you will feel it for yourself. Its future is brighter than a daisy.

Mahalia on Records
Selected Discography

Bless This House. Columbia Records CL 899, CS 8761
"Let the Church Roll On," "God Knows the Reason Why," "Standing Here Wondering Which Way to Go," "By His Word," "Trouble of the World," "Bless This House," "It Don't Cost Very Much," "Summertime," "Sometimes I Feel Like a Motherless Child," "Just a Little While to Stay Here," "Take My Hand, Precious Lord," "Down by the Riverside," "The Lord's Prayer"

Come On, Children, Let's Sing. Columbia CL 1428, CS 8225
"Come On, Children, Let's Sing," "If We Never Needed the Lord Before," "Because His Name Is Jesus," "You Must Be Born Again," "Brown Baby," "The Christian's Testimony," "Keep a-Movin'," "A Christian Duty," "One Step," "God Is So Good"

Great Gettin' Up Morning. Columbia CL 1343, CS 8153
"Great Gettin' Up Morning," "How Great Thou Art," "I Found the Answer," "To Me It's Wonderful," "His," "God Put a Rainbow in the Sky," "He Must Have Known," "When I've Done My Best," "Just to Behold His Face," "My Journey to the Sky," "Tell the World About This"

Great Songs of Love and Faith. Columbia CL 1824, CS 8624
"Danny Boy," "The Green Leaves of Summer," "I've Done My Work," "The Rosary," "Crying in the Chapel," "A Perfect Day," "Because," "Whither Thou Goest," "Trees," "My Friend," "The House I Live In"

I Believe. Columbia CL 1549, CS 8349

"Trouble," "I Believe," "I'm Grateful," "I See God," "Holding My Saviour's Hand," "Somebody Bigger Than You and I," "I Asked the Lord," "I Hear Angels," "Always Look Up, Never Look Down"

Let's Pray Together. Columbia CL 2130, CS 8930

"Altar of Peace," "One God," "Let's Pray Together," "Without a Song," "Take God by the Hand," "Guardian Angels," "We Shall Overcome," "Song for My Brother," "Deep River," "No Night There," "If I Can Help Somebody"

Mahalia Sings. Columbia CL 2452, CS 9252

"Rusty Bells," "Like the Breeze Blows," "Somewhere Listening," "Shall I Become a Castaway," "Jesus Is the Light," "I Thought of You and Said a Little Prayer," "Sunrise, Sunset," "Just a Closer Walk with Thee," "He Is Here," "God Speaks," "This Old Building," "The Velvet Rose"

Mahalia Jackson—The World's Greatest Gospel Singer and the Falls-Jones Ensemble. Columbia CL 644, CS 8759

"I'm Going to Live the Life I Sing About in My Song," "When I Wake Up in Glory," "Jesus Met the Woman at the Well," "Oh Lord, It Is I," "I Will Move On Up a Little Higher," "When the Saints Go Marching In," "Jesus," "Out of the Depths," "Walk over God's Heaven," "Keep Your Hand on the Plow," "Didn't It Rain"

Mahalia Jackson's Greatest Hits. Columbia CL 2004, CS 8804

"Walk in Jerusalem," "The Upper Room," "He Calmed the Ocean," "It Is No Secret," "How I Got Over," "Then the Answer Came," "Just over the Hill," "That's What He's Done for Me," "Move On Up a Little Higher," "Nobody Knows the Trouble I've Seen"

Make a Joyful Noise unto the Lord. Columbia CL 1936, CS 8736

"Sign of the Judgment," "That's All Right," "He Is Beside Me," "In Times Like These," "I Couldn't Keep It to Myself," "It's in My Heart," "No Other Help I Know," "It Took a Miracle," "Without God I Could Do Nothing," "Speak, Lord Jesus," "Lord, Don't Let Me Fail"

Newport 1958. Columbia CL 1244, CS 8071

"An Evening Prayer," "I'm on My Way," "A City Called Heaven," "It Don't Cost Very Much," "Walk Over God's Heaven," "The Lord's Prayer," "Didn't It Rain," "My God Is Real," "He's Got the Whole World in His Hands," "I'm Going to Live the Life I Sing About in My Song," "Joshua Fit the Battle of Jericho," "His Eye Is on the Sparrow"

The Power and the Glory. Columbia CL 1473, CS 8264; tapes: CQ 326, RCQ 7

"Onward, Christian Soldiers," "The Holy City," "Holy, Holy, Holy," "In the Garden," "Just as I Am," "Rock of Ages," "Lift Up Your Heads," "My Country, 'Tis of Thee," "The Lord Is My Light," "Jesus, Saviour, Pilot Me," "Nearer, My God, to Thee," "Abide with Me"

Recorded in Europe During Her Last Concert Tour. Columbia CL 1726, CS 8526

"Tell the World About This," "There Is a Balm in Gilead," "Down by the Riverside," "In My Home over There," "He's Right on Time," "Eliah Rock," "It Don't Cost Very Much," "You'll Never Walk Alone," "How I Got Over"

Silent Night—Songs for Christmas. Columbia CL 1903, CS 8703

"Sweet Little Jesus Boy," "A Star Stood Still," "Hark, the Herald Angels Sing," "Christmas Comes to Us All Once a Year," "Joy to the World," "O Come, All Ye Faithful," "O Little Town of Bethlehem," "What Can I Give," "Go Tell It on the Mountain," "Silent Night, Holy Night"

Sweet Little Jesus Boy. CL 702

"Silent Night, Holy Night," "No Room at the Inn," "O Little Town of Bethlehem," "The Holy Babe," "Joy to the World," "O Come, All Ye Faithful," "Go Tell It on the Mountain," "White Christmas," "I Wonder As I Wander," "Sweet Little Jesus Boy"

You'll Never Walk Alone. Columbia CL 2552

"Trouble in My Way," "Down by the Riverside," "You're not Living in Vain," "Without a Song," "Joshua Fit the Battle of Jericho," "You'll Never Walk Alone"

The Co-Author and
the Book

EVAN MCLEOD WYLIE was born in 1916, and majored in English literature at the University of Virginia. His extensive writing credits include several movie and television scripts, and hundreds of articles in the nation's leading magazines, on subjects ranging from medicine and religion to travel and crime. He has done magazine profiles on puppeteers Bil and Cora Baird and on Henry Fonda, among many others. Mahalia Jackson and he decided to work together on her autobiography after he had interviewed her for a *Saturday Evening Post* article.

MOVIN' ON UP is the result of a collaboration which carried Mr. Wylie across the continent, to Miss Jackson's Chicago home and New Orleans birthplace, to Music Inn in the Berkshires and to concert halls and recording studios. A song by Mahalia Jackson can still send shivers down his spine, Mr. Wylie says.

Evan Wylie lives in New York City with his wife and three sons.

MOVIN' ON UP was set into type by Pyramid Composition Co., printed by Halliday Lithographic Corp., and bound by American Book-Stratford Press. The text type is Caledonia, one of the most popular general-purpose book faces. It was created by the pre-eminent type and book designer, William Addison Dwiggins. The chapter titles are set in Ultra Bodoni, an eccentric face adapted from Bodoni types by Morris Benton in 1924.

A HAWTHORN BOOK